THE
COMING
SHIFT

LARRY RANDOLPH

THE COMING SHIFT

LARRY RANDOLPH

MorningStar Publications

A DIVISION OF MORNINGSTAR FELLOWSHIP CHURCH

375 Star Light Drive, Fort Mill, SC 29715

The Coming Shift
Copyright © 2006 by Larry Randolph

Distributed by MorningStar Publications, Inc., a division of MorningStar
Fellowship Church, 375 Star Light Drive, Fort Mill, SC 29715

International Standard Book Number: 978-1-59933-0440; 1-59933-044-X

MorningStar's website: www.morningstarministries.org
For information call 1-800-542-0278.

Larry Randolph Ministries
P.O. Box 157, Moravian Falls, NC 28654-0157
Website: www.larryrandolph.com / E-mail: Info@larryrandolph.com
For information call: (336) 921-4447

Cover design by
Book layout by Dana Zondory

Contents

DEDICATION

This book is dedicated to the men and women throughout church history who have found the courage to change. At extreme costs to their lives and ministries, many have chosen the road less traveled, enduring the disapproval and criticism of the "status quo."

One such man of change is my spiritual father, Hollis Vaughn. Thank you, Hollis—for modeling for me the lost art of change and transition. Although you seldom chose the easy way, I have always been impressed with your willingness to follow the convictions of your heart—even at the cost of painful isolation. Your love for spiritual transformation has truly inspired me to loathe my addiction to convenience and embrace the often difficult, but necessary winds of change.

I am also thankful for the many spiritual truths you have taught me throughout the years. Whether it seemed like it or not, I was always listening and learning. In fact, one of the most life-changing things I learned from you is the reality that "ultimate truth never changes, but our *perception* of that truth changes under daily observation." Because of this revelation, I made a commitment many years ago to pursue the challenge in II Corinthians 3:18, to live a life of transformation—from glory to glory to glory.

By no means have I achieved this lofty goal, but thank God, the Holy Spirit used you to put me on this path. Although I have stumbled along the way, I can't imagine where my life and ministry would be without the perseverance of a spiritual father willing to encourage me for who I am, but equally determined to provoke me to change. My heart is also humbled by the love of a God who refuses to leave me unchanged. For all these things, I am most grateful.

OPENING THOUGHTS

As a young man, one of my greatest worries was that God would do something new and not tell me. I so disliked being out of the loop of things that I frequently stayed awake all night long in fear that something spectacular might happen, and I would miss it. Many nights I prayed until the early hours of the morning, anticipating a fresh visitation from the Lord.

To this day, I still yearn for what "can be" and get a little nervous around people who are content to live for the moment. Maybe it is my prophetic nature that attracts me to the future, or just the fact that I am an adventurous dreamer. I am not really sure, but I agree with Thomas Jefferson who said, *"I like the dreams of the future better than the history of the past."* That being the case, my heart often beats with anticipation for that which is yet to come.

Also, as a result of my fixation on the future, I find it difficult to embrace much of the religious repetition that is related to yesterday's glory. I understand that Hebrews 13:8 portrays Jesus as being the same today and tomorrow as He was yesterday. And I deeply appreciate the passage in Revelation 1:8 which states that God **"is"** and **"was"** and is **"yet to come."** But, I really think it's the *"yet to come"* that keeps me sane in a world that is boringly predictable and stuck in a mindset of "what is" and "what has been."

For these reasons, my continual prayer is that I can position myself for the fulfillment of my tomorrow. On occasion, I take inventory of my life and ministry and ask God to reveal any area where I am lagging behind. Frequently, the Lord visits me and reveals the obstacles that jeopardize my journey, as well as the changes and shifts that lie ahead. He has also been faithful to inform me about seasons of coming revival in the church.

The Big Shift

In 1987, for example, Jesus informed me about the spiritual renewal that began in Canada in the beginning of 1994. He showed me the ramifications of this outpouring and graciously allowed me to participate in the early stages of the renewal.

At the turn of the new millennium, however, the Lord visited me once again and talked to me about the current status of renewal in America. He let me know that the initial wave had passed and we were in the eye of the storm. He explained that a "greater release" was coming that would reshape the face of modern Christianity.

Several years later, the Lord further informed me that this "greater release" would be in the form of a spiritual earthquake which would erupt into a mighty revival. In that day, the Lord said He will shake everything that can be shaken and only that which cannot be shaken will remain (see Haggai 2:6).

As I pondered these things, I was reminded that the shaking and rumbling of a natural earthquake is actually the result of a shift of the tectonic plates beneath the crust of the earth. I was further reminded that the same thing is true in a spiritual sense—especially pertaining to the revival that is coming.

In this context, I began to see the many adjustments necessary to accommodate the next move of God. I saw how ridiculous it would be to believe for a fresh outpouring of God's Spirit and not be willing to change both in a practical and theological sense. I came to understand that people and churches not designed with the flexibility to shift will find it difficult to transition into the next move of God.

Finally, a crystal-clear revelation regarding change came in the fall of 2004. In the month of October, I was awakened in the middle of the night with a sense of urgency. At that point, the words of John 21 began to resonate in my spirit like an echo in a great valley.

I was familiar with this particular passage and had put a lot of thought into the story of Peter's legendary fishing trip. I knew that after Christ's death, the disheartened disciple returned to his former trade as a fisherman. I also knew that the resurrected Lord appeared to the weary disciple after an unsuccessful night of fishing and commanded him to cast his net on the other side of the boat. The result was a miraculous catch of fish.

In spite of my familiarity with the spiritual parallels in John 21, the Lord spoke a word that pierced my heart. It was simple, but challenging. He said, "Like Peter, you have been fishing from the wrong side of the boat." He also let me know that scores of other Christians are struggling with the same issue, and challenged me to closely examine this story and pass on the new truths I would soon discover.

The following morning, I went on a journey to discover *when* and *how* I had been fishing from the wrong side of the boat. Over the next few days, the Holy Spirit revealed to me seven ways to identify when I was fishing from the *wrong* side of the boat and seven ways to tell when I was fishing from the *right* side of the boat.

The message was clear. The church today cannot expect a fresh encounter with the supernatural until we seriously evaluate which side of the boat we are fishing from. As I mentioned earlier, there may not be a "next move of God" for many of us unless there is a dramatic shift in the way we conduct our lives and ministries. Old paradigms of thinking must die; new vision must be embraced. Practically speaking, the difference between success and failure for many will be determined by a willingness to accommodate change.

A Rich Legacy

Before I attempt to lay out the thesis for change and transition in this book, I want to acknowledge the many manifestations of revival in the recent past. I am fully aware that millions of people around the world have had significant encounters with the Spirit of God. Actually, some of the greatest missionaries, churches, and church leaders have been raised up during these times. On a global scale, the overall advance of Christianity has been unprecedented since the turn of the first century.

Also, in the Western Hemisphere there have been significant revivals over the last one hundred years. In America alone, God has poured out His Spirit in a way that is astonishing. As I see it, this nation has experienced three successive waves of spiritual renewal in the twentieth century which are unparalleled by anything in church history.

The first wave on January 1, 1901 began with Charles Parham's Bethel Bible School in Topeka, Kansas. The subsequent outpouring of the Holy Spirit of 1906, at Azusa Street in Los Angeles, also led to the expansion of God's kingdom throughout many countries. This renewal founded by William Seymour was alive with spiritual gifts and the miraculous power of the Holy Spirit. Numerous men and women demonstrated the healing power of God, along with prophetic signs and wonders. There were enormous crusades, tent revivals, dramatic preaching, and other exhibitions of ministry relevant to the culture of that day. Out of this revival emerged eleven thousand classical Pentecostal denominations, which grew to over 360 million members by the beginning of the third millennium.

The second wave of "Neo-Pentecostal" power hit the historic Protestant and Roman Catholic churches in the

1960s. This outpouring of the Spirit, referred to as the Charismatic Renewal, began in 1960 with Dennis Bennett, an Episcopal rector in Van Nuys, California, and eventually spread to 55 million Protestants worldwide. Also, the Catholic Charismatic Renewal that began in 1967, in Pittsburgh, Pennsylvania, among students and faculty of Duquesne University, touched the lives of over 80 million Catholics in over 120 nations. To the surprise of many, the Holy Spirit was introduced to other mainline churches, resulting in a cross-denominational outpouring of God's power. In a few short decades, the renewal reached "critical mass," and untold millions of non-Pentecostals received the baptism of the Holy Spirit.

Finally, the third wave of renewal in the latter part of the twentieth century is often linked to John Wimber's ministry at Fuller Theological Seminary, beginning around 1981. This outpouring touched a vast number of non-Charismatics in both mainline and independent churches throughout the world. The emphasis seemed to be centered on the supernatural power of God in the form of divine healing and miracles. Experts like George Barna, the president of the Barna Research Group based in Ventura, California, say that by 1990, a total of 33 million people in the world were moving in signs and wonders, though they did not carry the Pentecostal or Charismatic label.

Honor

It has been said that all three of these renewals together have produced more salvations, more people baptized in the Holy Spirit, more missionaries being sent out, and more churches being birthed, than all previous moves of God combined! Indeed, the statistics are staggering. In America today, Barna says that 80 million Christians attend independent churches and 43 percent of the recognized church membership considers themselves part of the Holy Spirit renewal movement. This does not include the other 500 million Christians worldwide who Barna says are associated with some form of Holy Spirit renewal. Also, James Rutz, the author of the widely acclaimed book *Mega Shift,* states that 707 million people around the world confess to be born-again, and the number is increasing by 8 percent per year.

Now that's fruit! And, for these things I commend those who have taken up the mandate of Christ to influence every culture and nation with the gospel of Christianity. I am also impressed with the estimate by Barna and other researchers that over one billion people have come to Christ during the last century. It also staggers my imagination to hear people like Rutz say that three thousand people around the globe are saved every twenty-five minutes. *"By tomorrow, there will be 175,000 more Christians than there are today,"* he writes.

In light of the overwhelming evidence, it would be shameful to ignore the incredible fruit of past and present revivals. On the contrary, this generation owes a great debt to the contribution made by classical Pentecostals, mainline Protestants, and Catholics, as well as the many para-church ministries and independent organizations that have furthered the cause of Christ through renewal. We must honor the people and movements that have paid the price for spiritual reformation and also respect the many orthodox denominations that are faithfully spreading the gospel through social and political venues.

Moving Forward

Am I suggesting that all is well with the church, and that we should be content with where we are presently? Absolutely not! As I mentioned in the beginning, I believe there is an unprecedented wave of revival on the horizon that will forever change the spiritual landscape of Christianity. With this in mind, I feel compelled to inform believers about the necessary changes that will accommodate this next outpouring of God's Spirit.

However, the fact that I am writing a book on change does not mean I have personally made the proper adjustments and preparations for the next move of God. In no way do I have all the answers, nor have I fully addressed the issues in my own life that limit my capacity for change.

Clearly, I am caught in transition, trying to hold in balance the tension between honoring yesterday's move of God and reaching out for greater dimensions of revival. Even so, my hope is that the church today can somehow incorporate the values of yesterday's glory into our spiritual foundation, and at the same time build a spiritual house that will accommodate the coming outpouring of the Holy Spirit.

In light of this reality, the following pages are dedicated to the shifts and changes necessary to transition into a new era of revival. Also, for better readability and flow of thought, the chapters in this book are not in chronological order with the events of John 21.

Simon Peter, and Thomas called Didymus, and Nathanael of Cana in Galilee, and the sons of Zebedee, and two other of His disciples were together.

Simon Peter said to them, "I am going fishing." They said to Him, "We will also come with you." They went out and got into the boat; and that night they caught nothing.

But when the day was now breaking, Jesus stood on the beach; yet the disciples did not know that it was Jesus.

So Jesus said to them, "Children, you do not have any fish, do you?" They answered Him, "No."

And He said to them, "Cast the net on the right-hand side of the boat and you will find a catch." So they cast, and then they were not able to haul it in because of the great number of fish.

Therefore that disciple whom Jesus loved said to Peter, "It is the Lord." So when Simon Peter heard that it was the Lord, he put his

outer garment on (for he was stripped for work), and threw himself into the sea.

But the other disciples came in the little boat, for they were not far from the land, but about one hundred yards away, dragging the net full of fish.

So when they got out on the land, they saw a charcoal fire already laid and fish placed on it, and bread.

Jesus said to them, "Bring some of the fish which you have now caught."

Simon Peter went up and drew the net to land, full of large fish, a hundred and fifty-three; and although there were so many, the net was not torn.

Jesus said to them, "Come and have breakfast." None of the disciples ventured to question Him, "Who are You?" knowing that it was the Lord.

Jesus came and took the bread, and gave it to them, and the fish likewise.

This is now the third time that Jesus was manifested to the disciples, after He was raised from the dead (John 21:2-14).

PART ONE

HOW TO KNOW WHEN YOU ARE

FISHING FROM THE WRONG

SIDE OF THE BOAT

1

DIRECTION SHIFT

You Know You Are Fishing From the Wrong
Side of the Boat When Jesus Redirects Your
Attention Elsewhere!

**So Jesus said to them, "Children, you do
not have any fish, do you?" They answered
Him "No."**

**And He said to them, "Cast the net on the
right-hand side of the boat and you will find
a catch" (John 21:5-6).**

As described in my opening thoughts, Christians in
the past one hundred years have been blessed
with a rich heritage of revival and church-growth. Even
today, a great number of people around the world are
experiencing an unprecedented touch of the Holy Spirit.

However, I believe the universal body of Christ
has yet to reach her maximum potential for worldwide
revival. Just as Peter arrived at a personal and spiritual
impasse in John 21:1-3, after experiencing a season of
successful ministry with Jesus, we are also standing
at the threshold of great transition. And, for the most
part, our past success cannot compensate for our lack of
preparation today.

In light of this, I am convinced the message of
John 21 is foundational to the changes necessary for

the global impact of the gospel. Peter, for example, represents many believers who are fishing from the wrong side of the boat. He is typical of people who are dangerously overcommitted to past success, or those who are too weary to make the necessary adjustments to change. Whichever the case, like this disciple, few today have awareness of how much a shift in direction can impact their future.

Yet, one of Peter's redeeming qualities was his willingness to take a risk. Previously, in Matthew 14:29, Jesus had beckoned the disciple to step out of his boat in a raging storm and walk on top of the water. To the surprise of the other disciples, Peter obeyed the Lord and defied the laws of gravity. In spite of his shortcomings, this disciple seemed to understand the value of living outside of his comfort zone. He seemed determined to break through any limitations that might keep him from moving forward in the pursuit of destiny.

Like Peter, I, too, am realizing the incredible value of being a risk-taker. I have learned that the Christian life is shaped by the many course corrections and readjustments that come our way. As Peter discovered, following Jesus means one must live a life of risk and change. This is partly due to the fact that our passage in life is rarely etched in stone, nor is it mapped out for us ahead of time. Instead, we learn to trust that **"the steps of a man are established by the Lord..." (Psalms 37:23).**

Does this mean we should be indifferent about our attempt to walk out our destiny? Are we without personal responsibility for our actions or lack of action?

My spiritual father, Hollis Vaughn, once told me that the Christian journey is like the voyage of a great ship. He reminded me that a ship's rudder gives direction while the vessel is in motion, not while it sits in the port. In a similar way, he explained that the fulfillment of our destiny depends on our willingness to go forward in life, even when we are unsure of the proper direction.

The simple wisdom from Hollis was that we learn as we go and trust the unfolding of God's purpose in the process. Again, this does not mean we should be irresponsible with our purpose in life or disregard our past successes. It simply means we depend on the Holy Spirit to lead us forward in our journey. After all, He is portrayed in John 16:13 as the great Comforter—the One who comes along beside believers to guide us into our destiny. As we move ahead in life, He is eager to help us make the necessary adjustments and course corrections along the way.

Course Correction

The following approach to navigation is well-known in the space industry. When NASA sent Apollo I to the moon, for example, there was a series of navigational changes made along the way. A host of unknown factors warranted last-minute course corrections while the rocket was in flight. Now and then, the astronauts had to realign the path of the capsule with the flight plan.

More importantly, NASA did not direct the space capsule to where the moon was at the time of launch. Instead, they calculated where the moon would be when the satellite would arrive and plotted a course to that particular location. As a result, two fast-moving objects millions of miles apart came together due to an incredible feat of variable navigation.

This same principle of navigation loosely applies to the spiritual journey of those traveling on the pathway of spiritual renewal. If we want to reach our potential in Christ, then we, must make the necessary adjustments that will align us with the fulfillment of our destiny. This includes significant changes in the way we think, live, and conduct our ministries. As a result of these shifts and changes, we will be better equipped to reach our destination.

Does this mean that we abandon our initial flight plan? Of course not! It would be foolish to begin a significant journey without plotting a course. Then again, it is equally foolish to stick to a preset program and not accommodate the necessary adjustments along the way. In the case of NASA, they were prepared for the trip ahead of time, but were flexible enough to make any navigational changes that might help complete the mission.

Skating to the Puck

A great hockey player was asked about the secret of his success. He replied, *"I don't skate to where the puck is; I skate to where the puck is going next."*

This athlete knew two things about the anatomy of success. First, through extensive training he had learned it is not always about the performance of the moment, but about positioning one's self for the next play. Next, experience had taught him the value of following his instincts, even though others might think he was going in the wrong direction. As a result of his commitment to these basic values, he was able to out-maneuver player after player and frequently score the winning goal.

This discipline is equally important to the success of athletes in other sports. For example, in the game of football, the wide receiver is rigorously trained to run to the spot where the ball will be thrown, not to where the ball is at the moment. His ultimate goal is to position himself down the field in anticipation of the coming throw. If he focuses on the ball in the hands of the quarterback, the success of the whole team is in jeopardy.

The same is true of believers who desire to catch the next wave of God's Spirit. We, too, cannot afford to live for the "now" but must position ourselves for the "future play." This means we must break out of the box of momentary glory and transition through the veil of tomorrow. When we make this shift, tomorrow's opportunity will become today's reality.

On a personal level, I have found these truths to be invaluable to my spiritual success. Because my vision is fixed toward the future, I have been able to maintain a measure of relevancy in my ministry. Intuitively, I have learned to skate to where the Holy Spirit is going, long before the current move of God reaches its peak. I am careful not to form an unhealthy connection to any particular spot in a spiritual river that is ever changing in dimension and velocity. This mindset has allowed me to minister on the ground floor of several significant revivals, giving me the courage to move on when a particular revival reaches maximum velocity and begins to decline.

Recognizing Change

As I have abundantly stated, the Christian journey is a pathway filled with crucial changes and course corrections. We often learn as we go and make the necessary shifts along the way. Generally speaking, the difference between success and failure is determined by a willingness to accommodate change. In other words, it is not the strongest Christian that succeeds, or the most intelligent, but the one most responsive to change.

This reality is also relevant to people outside the walls of the church. Actually, the Christian community can learn a lot from the successes and failures of those in the secular world. This is especially true of business people and companies that have to deal with the many changes in a world market which is constantly evolving.

In the middle of the twentieth century, for example, the Swiss were world leaders in the manufacturing of watches. Switzerland was home to famous world-class timepieces. They prided themselves in the design and manufacturing of the springs, gears, bearings, and other mechanical parts that were characteristic of the famous "Swiss movement." By the 1960s, the Swiss owned 50 percent of the world market share for watches and over 90 percent of the industry's profit. In light of this success, there seemed to be little need for change.

In the latter part of that decade, however, a Swiss researcher invented a quartz watch with electronic movement. Unlike the mechanical watch, it was amazingly accurate and required very little upkeep. When it was presented to the Swiss Watch Board, they rejected the research on the belief that people would not buy a watch without gears and moving parts. They failed to see the need for such new technology and refused to apply for a patent.

Frustrated by the decision, the Swiss researcher demonstrated his watch in a trade show the following year. A representative of an American electronics company named Texas Instruments and a certain Mr. Seiko from Japan happened to see the new technology and seized the opportunity. They saw the future of watch making and began to manufacture and market the quartz watch worldwide.

Unknowingly, the Swiss handed over their watch making future to others willing to embrace change. By the 1980s, the electronic watch dominated the industry and the Swiss ownership of the market had plummeted drastically. Today, the Swiss own less than 3 percent of the global sales for their world-class timepieces.

Flexibility

Change eventually knocks on everyone's door. The question is: Will we answer the call or will we hide in the comfort zone of that which is familiar?

If the success of our future lies in our ability to recognize change, then we must, at all cost, change. When change knocked at the door of the Swiss watch industry, they held to the familiar. On the contrary, those willing to take a risk recognized the future in something that seemed too far out of the box for its time. They understood that new paradigms usually show up long before they are needed.

In this same vein of thought, the great Albert Einstein said, *"the definition of insanity is doing the same thing over and over again and expecting different results."* Someone else also said that the first sign of insanity is blind commitment to a lifetime of absolutes without ever entertaining the possibility of change.

Like these men, I have discovered that flexibility is a valuable friend. I have learned to let go of things that I believe are of little consequence. Of course there is absolute truth in God's kingdom that I consider non-negotiable. However, the only thing I am totally absolute about in life's journey is to never be totally absolute.

Also, every time I think I have figured out my future, the Lord seems to rearrange my tomorrow. He begins by stirring my nest of comfortable dreams and preparing me for the next phase of my flight. I am forever dependent on the daily guidance of the Holy Spirit in my life. If I lag behind, He urges me forward. If I run too far ahead of my destiny, He pulls me back.

Closing Thoughts

Overall, I have learned to be pliable. Like the Swiss watch people, I now understand that the success of my tomorrow depends on my flexibility today. Simply put, my past achievements, no matter how wonderful they have been, serve only as stepping stones to a greater future. This means, my willingness to change and let go of the past gives God an opportunity to trust me with new paradigms of success.

Is it possible to invoke this level of change when and where we desire? Can we initiate these transitions at our own discretion?

As sons and daughters of God, we have been empowered as agents of change. Also, Jesus clearly stated in Matthew 17:20 that all things are possible to them that believe. With these two things in mind, it is extremely easy for me to believe that with the help of the Holy Spirit believers can experience fresh paradigms of change.

However, as I will illustrate in the next chapter, there is an appropriate time and season for everything in creation. Knowing this, change is more beneficial when we synchronize our efforts with the current purpose of God on the earth. This is done in part by knowing when a particular season is over and when it is time to embrace new opportunities. In order to make a clean transition, we need an awareness of the time we are living in and a clear vision for the next step of our destiny.

QUESTIONS TO CONSIDER

- Am I flexible, or do I stubbornly stick to that which is familiar?
- Am I willing to make the necessary course corrections that will re-align me with my destiny?
- In what ways can I position myself for the future?

SCRIPTURES TO PONDER

But we all with unveiled face . . . are being transformed into the same image from glory to glory . . . (II Corinthians 3:18).

...we will not all sleep, but we will all be changed (I Corinthians 15:51).

Therefore if anyone is in Christ, he is a new creature; the old things passed away; behold, new things have come (II Corinthians 5:17).

SEASON SHIFT

> **You Know You Are Fishing From the Wrong Side of the Boat When You Are More Committed to Yesterday's Lure Than to Today's Catch!**

And He (Jesus) said to them, "Cast the net on the right-hand side of the boat...." So they cast, and then they were not able to haul it in because of the great number of fish (John 21:6).

Like Peter, I grew up with a deep love for fishing. Most of my time was spent going from one farm pond to another looking for the perfect "fishing hole." When pond fishing did not produce favorable results, I would walk the many creeks surrounding my hometown in search of that elusive school of fish.

I just could not help myself. Visions of big fish lurking at the bottom of murky water greatly intrigued me. I was insanely addicted to the smell of stinky fish, never tiring of the thrill that this sport provided. Rain or shine, I would be standing at the edge of a pond, or on the bank of a creek, in earnest expectation of catching the "big one."

As I grew older, I discovered several things that made me a better fisherman. I learned that fishing is not a game of luck, but a blend of careful planning and know-how. I quickly discovered the importance of using the right lure, at the right time, in the right season. As with any conquest in life, I learned that it takes know-how to maintain a consistent level of success.

I learned, for example, that in the springtime spawning fish usually strike a plastic worm or jig that is dragged slowly over their spawning bed. In the fall, they seem to respond more positively to other types of lures and will bite anything you put in the water. Other times, you can throw the whole tackle box at them and catch nothing.

At any rate, I know better than to fish without careful consideration of the proper procedures that are appropriate for a specific time of the year. Of course, it is tempting to throw my favorite lure year-round. But I have learned that the same lure, which brought me success in an earlier season, can now be a waste of time. In order to catch fish, I must use the bait compatible with the season in which I am fishing.

Yesterday's Success

Yesterday's success can quickly become today's disappointment. It seems Peter had to deal with this truth throughout much of his life. In fact, his early success as a career fisherman ended the day he met Jesus of Nazareth and began to follow His ministry. And at the end of those three glorious years, he went back to his old ways, but could not produce the positive results he enjoyed earlier. Everything he did seemed out of sync with his present reality.

The children of Israel learned this lesson the hard way. In Exodus 16:20, God gave them manna to eat in the wilderness and instructed them not to leave any over for the next day. When they disobeyed and tried to eat what they had gathered the day before, the outcome was most unpleasant. They quickly discovered that yesterday's manna breeds today's worms.

Perhaps these things were in Peter's mind when he praised the church in II Peter 1:12 for being **"...established in the present truth"** (NKJV). King Solomon also understood the value of living in present truth and wrote in Ecclesiastes 3:1, that there is a season and time for every purpose under the sun. Although both men knew that truth is absolute, they also understood that the unfolding of truth to mankind is progressive.

To put it another way, the perception and application of truth changes from one season of life to another. For example, a mother's womb provides a vital place of nourishment for a growing infant. During the nine months of formation and growth, it is the safest place in the world for the baby. The environment in the womb is specifically designed to meet every need of the child and prepare it for the next stage of life.

Even so, if the infant stays beyond its time and does not make the transition out of the womb, the situation becomes critical. Yesterday's place of nourishment becomes today's tomb. What was good for the baby in one season of its life, is now a threat. If the baby does not make the shift, it will eventually die.

The same thing is true of the metamorphosis of a butterfly. The drama begins when the caterpillar weaves a cocoon out of its own body. It then hibernates in the cocoon where it is transformed into an embryonic butterfly. Then when the transformed butterfly is ready, it breaks through the cocoon to a new stage of life.

Like the infant in the womb, the butterfly will also die if it does not make the proper transition from the cocoon. Also, if you try to help either the baby or butterfly transition before their time, you will jeopardize their chance for a normal transition. In both cases, it is the natural process of metamorphosis that produces a favorable outcome.

Renewal Metamorphosis

The principle of metamorphosis also applies to the move of God in a spiritual sense. Throughout the church's history, we have gone through a challenging process of renewal transformation. There have been many renewals and revivals that have come and gone. We have also experienced spiritual revolutions, which have transformed the way we do church. And, every now and then, an earthshaking reformation comes along and challenges the very core of our theology.

Why the need for this constant cycle of spiritual evolution? Why is it necessary to transition from one cocoon of renewal to another?

First, we must understand that there is only one Lord, one Spirit, and one river of spiritual revival that flows through the body of Christ. Although this river has taken many twists and turns throughout the history of Christianity, its origin and life are indigenous to the Holy Spirit. Thus, true moves of the Spirit, no matter how diverse they may seem, have at their cellular level the DNA of God and are true reflections of the Father's heart.

However, when a move of God begins to grow in visibility, men have a tendency to tarnish its image through acts of self-interest. The more it is handled by human hands, the more it is changed from God's original intent. That which was created in God's image takes on the image of the creation instead of the Creator. Eventually, the Holy Spirit is grieved and forms a fresh embryo of renewal that will carry the church into another season of spiritual growth.

On the other hand, there are spiritual movements that keep their original purity, but still go through a normal process of spiritual transformation. Like the developing infant in the womb or the evolving butterfly, there is a genetic code written in the DNA of revival that helps it make the transition from one stage of growth to another. Unlike a move of God that is prematurely forced out of its incubation stage, these renewals evolve in appearance and purpose through a process of spiritual metamorphosis. When God's purpose is served for that particular moment in time, the renewal makes a critical transition.

From Glory to Glory

Whether from abortion or a process of metamorphosis, one thing is certain: The church is in a constant state of transition, from one season of renewal to another. As stated in the first chapter, there have been three major waves of renewal in the twentieth century. Throughout this time, smaller manifestations of renewal, commonly known as "movements," have emerged in North America. In my own lifetime, I have experienced the rise and decline of several of these movements, and will address them briefly. Because they overlapped in time, however, the following list is not exhaustive or in precise chronological order.

In the 1960s, during the transition from Pentecostal Renewal to Charismatic Renewal, the Jesus Movement came on the scene and reshaped the spiritual landscape of religion. The Holy Spirit was once again introduced to the church, but in a different cultural package. This time the beneficiaries were a generation of troubled youth in search of life's meaning. Multitudes of hippies and drug addicts came to church and were deeply touched by the power of the Holy Spirit. However, there was an emphasis-shift in the Spirit and the movement began to decrease.

The Word of Faith Movement also became popular in the early 1970s. This movement was a great counterbalance for the lack of biblical foundations that plagued the previous movement. It emphasized the power of the spoken word for physical healing and financial prosperity. Through faith and positive confession of Scripture, people found deliverance from spirits of poverty and negativism. Even so, the movement eventually reached a spiritual plateau and seemed to lose momentum.

By the mid 1970s, the Deliverance Movement had also peaked in popularity. It was extremely useful in its pure form and provided help for those oppressed by evil spirits. Many people found freedom from mental torment, depression, suicidal spirits, family curses, and other forms of evil influences. It, too, was short-lived in popularity and the emphasis of many Bible teachers shifted from authority over evil spirits to other aspects of kingdom life.

Around that time, the Shepherding Movement greatly impacted believers around the world. This particular movement confronted the spirit of independence, which had infiltrated the church during the late 1960s and early 1970s. There was also a much-needed emphasis on governmental authority and submission to church leadership. Like the Deliverance Movement, however, it enjoyed a brief season of popularity, but went through a turbulent season of criticism and experienced a rapid decline.

Another spiritual phenomenon, known as the Kingdom Now Movement, caught the attention of many in the late 1970s and early 1980s. The main focus was centered on the premise that God's kingdom is happening now, not later. There was a theological shift that redirected our focus from experiencing God in the sweet by-and-by, to experiencing heaven on earth today. After a short engagement, it was beset with great controversy and practically disappeared from the scene.

In the early 1980s, the Spiritual Warfare Movement drew attention to a believer's right to wage war against wicked spirits. We were taught that a believer's struggle was not with mortal men as stated in Ephesians 6:12, but against principalities and powers, in high places. Subsequently, a new breed of shofar blowing, sword swinging intercessors emerged from their prayer closets with an emphasis on banner-waving and pageantry which they believed were symbolic acts of warfare against the devil. After experiencing great opposition from the dark side, the movement began to diminish in popularity.

By the turn of the 1980s, the Apostolic and Prophetic Movements began to emerge in the nation. Certain apostles were endorsed as being the unchallenged leaders in the hierarchy of the church, and great emphasis was placed on their authority to rule over geographical regions and groups of people. Also, the gift of prophecy was reinstated as a core value in the body of Christ, and the prophet's ministry was recognized as a legitimate part of church government. However, the movement was not widely received in the church and went through an extended cooling-off period.

In the early 1990s, the Laughter Movement (a spin-off of the Third Wave Renewal) swept a number of countries with incredible force. New life was breathed into the lungs of weary Christians in the form of laughter, spiritual drunkenness, and other phenomenal manifestations. People were gloriously set free from their inhibitions and found fresh ways to express their hearts to God. However, much of the phenomena associated with the movement came under scrutiny by religious conservatives, and by the turn of the new millennium, many associated with the movement began to transition into a more seeker-sensitive form of Christianity.

Old Landmarks

Now for the application of our metaphor about fishing out of season! How do we relate practically to these past moves of God? And, what can we learn from a half-century of evolving revival?

First, I want to commend the wonderful men and women of God who pioneered these movements. Even though their message was often misunderstood, many of them received an original blueprint for renewal that was unique to their generation. Actually, a great number of them still carry an authority for that revelation today.

In my view, most of the problems that occurred did not lie primarily with the founders, but with those in the lower ranks of the movement. Since many believers did not possess the revelation of the founding fathers of the movement, there was often a distortion of the original vision. Therefore, the purpose of that particular renewal was misinterpreted and misapplied. These misrepresentations eventually damaged the incubation time of the movement and created a premature transition from its spiritual cocoon.

However, this was not the case with other moves of God. As stated earlier, several movements simply fulfilled God's purpose in their season and experienced a transformation in appearance. Although they were divinely conceived, they were eventually phased out by the Holy Spirit. Unlike the movements that died from self-destruction, they fell prey to divine intervention.

In either event, the fact remains that we should respect the past moves of God. According to Proverbs 22:28, true sons honor the ancient landmarks set by their fathers. In this frame of mind, we must incorporate the spiritual fiber of past revivals into our spiritual foundation and recognize that the core values of yesterday's moves of God are essential for an emerging generation of new believers.

On the other hand, while honoring the accomplishments of our spiritual forefathers, we must be careful not to fashion the present move of God in the exact image of past revival. As with the infant and the butterfly, yesterday's place of incubation can easily become today's death trap. In essence, we jeopardize our potential for creativity when we measure our future by the magnitude of yesterday's phenomena. In all of its glory, yesterday is still yesterday and can never replace the need for God's presence today.

Closing Thoughts

With regard to these things, how then do we hold in balance the tension between that which is, and was, and is *"yet to come?"* How do we strike the critical balance between honoring the glory of the past and embracing the glory of the future?

As previously indicated, this generation is privileged to tap into the ancient wells of past renewals. Yet, successful men and women of God remain successful by saying and doing what God is currently saying and doing. This means we bless what heaven is blessing today and try not to live in yesterday. We honor the past, but strive to press forward into our destiny—from one season of glory to another.

Generally speaking, we cannot afford to hold tight to a passing season of renewal and miss the dawning of God's destiny for our lives. Neither can we wrap ourselves in the cocoon of yesterday's experience and expect to catch the coming wave of the Spirit. We must "fish with the lure" that is compatible with the season in which we live. If not, we will continue to labor from the unproductive side of life when the Lord is calling us to cast our nets on the other side.

QUESTIONS TO CONSIDER

- Am I jeopardizing my future by hanging on to past glory? How so?
- Has yesterday's place of nourishment become a spiritual death trap?
- Am I open to transition and change, or am I in a place of spiritual stagnation?

SCRIPTURES TO PONDER

...but one thing I do: forgetting what lies behind and reaching forward to what lies ahead (Philippians 3:13).

Behold, I will do something new; now it will spring forth...(Isaiah 43:19).

There is an appointed time for everything. And there is a time for every event under heaven (Ecclesiastes 3:1).

3
SOUL SHIFT

> You Know You Are Fishing From the
> Wrong Side of the Boat When Hope Is
> Replaced by Disappointment and Despair

Simon Peter said to them, "I am going fishing." They said to him, "We will also come with you" (John 21:3).

As illustrated in the previous two chapters, Peter represents believers who are faced with the harsh reality of change. His situation is also typical of the many uncertainties of life that come our way. Like many of us, when confronted by sweeping changes, this disciple seemed to be lost in a world that was constantly evolving. Just the previous day, he had been enjoying success, and now the world as he knew it had come to an end.

Why such an extreme shake-up in Peter's life? When hope dies, passion is soon to follow. When Jesus died on Calvary, Peter's hopes and dreams seemed to die with Him. Until that historic day, he was convinced that the Lord was going to be crowned king of Israel and that he would reign with Him. Now all that remained was the haunting echo of what seemed like a cruel and empty promise.

Everything in Peter's life had fallen apart. He had lost his Lord, his ministry, his faith and integrity, and now he couldn't produce a single fish after a long night of sweat and toil. Thankfully, he went forward in life, but not with the same zeal that motivated him in the past. Jesus had promised that he and the other disciples would become fishers of men, but once again they were fishing for fish. Passion was long gone and destiny seemed to be lost in the confusion of events that had recently transpired.

In what way does this apply to the lives of believers today? Although I do not have all the answers, I am sure of two things. First, I have found that comfortable people seldom change. It's just too painful. They change only when the pain of their present condition is greater than the pain it takes to change. For this reason, God is often reluctant to deliver us from hurtful situations, and will often allow us to simmer in our discomfort until we are forced to cry out for transformation. As with Peter, the pain of failure and disillusionment became the tipping point for change and provided the disciple with an opportunity to transition into a fresh dimension of God's purpose.

I am aware that many modern-day Christians have also suffered the death of their hopes and dreams. Perhaps we have misinterpreted the purpose of our destiny, or we are wrong about the timing. Or, maybe we have let the misfortunes of life steal a piece of our future dreams. In either event, many of us go through life fishing out of sheer habit instead of passion. And, once we give in to disappointment and despair, as with Peter, we bring others along with us, adding to the problem. Ultimately, we end up living our lives from a mindset of hopelessness.

In view of these things, I am certain of our need for radical change. If we want to fish from the productive side of the boat, we must be willing to shift even though feelings and circumstances tell us otherwise. If we ignore this call for change, success will elude our best attempts to fill our nets. Most importantly, we can miss our appointment with destiny.

Finding Hope in Despair

On a personal level, I have faced seasons of intense adversity. Some of these hardships diminished with the passing of time—others have been fatal to my hopes and dreams.

At one point in my life, I went through a season of tragedies and failures that seemed too difficult to bear. In the end, I was overcome with such a sense of loss that I gave up the struggle of full-time ministry and returned to the workplace. My hopes and dreams for fulfilling God's call on my life appeared to be lost forever, and like Peter, I was fishing out of disappointment.

After several years of this despair, the Lord visited me and encouraged my heart. He awakened me late one night and talked to me about the many discouragements that the Apostle Paul faced in his ministry.

"If anyone had a reason to despair," He said, "it was Paul." He informed me that this great apostle suffered from pain, hunger, thirst, and was at times cold and weary. He was also betrayed, beaten, put in prison, and eventually shipwrecked on a remote island (see Acts 14:19, II Corinthians 11:23-28).

All of this, the Lord said, was not because Paul was out of His will, but was actually a sign that the apostle was walking in His will. I was reminded that Jesus had revealed to Paul in Acts 9:16 the great things he must suffer for the Lord's sake. The Lord also reminded me that those who live godly lives in Christ will suffer persecution (see II Timothy 3:12).

Then Jesus spoke a simple word to my heart that forever shifted my outlook on life. He said, "The will of God is often met with great adversity." He exhorted me to never make the mistake of believing that His will is easy, or that it goes unchallenged by evil powers. He also informed me that in spite of my adversity I am blessed by the Father God **"...who according to His great mercy has caused us to be born again to a living hope through the resurrection of Jesus Christ from the dead" (I Peter 1:3).**

The next day, I made a quality decision to pull out of my pit of despair. If this was the case in Paul's life, I concluded, then why must it be any different for me? People in the Bible such as Abraham, Moses, David, and Joseph also faced incredible adversity but refused to bow their knees to a spirit of despair. They not only weathered the storms of life, but survived against impossible odds. In the end, hope guided them to the fulfillment of their destiny.

As a result of this revelation, I came to understand that the fulfillment of my dream is tied to my willingness to hope in the midst of despair. Regardless of my situation, I had to shift. I could not let my dream become a nightmare. Nor could I let the *illusion* of failure dictate my destiny. Regardless of the pain of the moment, I had to revive my passion for life. I could no longer fish from a paradigm of hopelessness.

Shortly after my encounter with the Lord things started to turn around. I found strength in the faith of the men previously mentioned and began to rediscover my zeal for ministry. Especially encouraging was the Romans 4:18 reference to Abraham, who in hope believed against hope. Within several years, I was free from the stranglehold of despair and once again I was swimming in the river of my destiny. Like Peter, pain and failure had brought me to the threshold of radical confrontation. This confrontation provoked change—change realigned me with my initial destiny.

The Big Shift

A God-given dream is the embryo of our destiny. Disappointment and despair, on the other hand, can be dream killers. If Satan can get you to abort your passion through hopelessness, he can steal your future. According to I Peter 5:8, he goes about like a thief seeking whom he can devour. He knows how important hope is to your purpose in life and will try to keep you in a prison of disappointment.

In spite of this evil strategy, we must never lose hope in God's ability to help us transition from the reality of His dream for us. Whether today or tomorrow, the Lord will make good on promises that are nurtured through faith and trust. We might have to shift our position now and then, but if we cling to hope, we will eventually see the fulfillment of our destiny.

These things were especially true for the life and ministry of Joseph. According to Genesis 37:5, the young lad was given a dream of wealth and power beyond his wildest imagination. However, after telling the dream, he was betrayed by his jealous brothers and sold into slavery. Rejected and falsely accused, he ended up in the bottom of an Egyptian prison for more than a decade.

Regardless of the misfortunes that befell the young dreamer, he never gave up hope. Psalm 105:19 says, **"until the time that his word came to pass, the word of the Lord tested him."** Because he was faithful to maintain a level of expectancy while in prison, God was faithful to fulfill his dream. And, when the fullness of time came, God enabled him to shift from a place of obscurity to a place of prosperity and rulership on Pharaoh's throne.

In what context does this incredible story apply to the present-day church? Like Joseph, believers today have been given an opportunity to transition from our "prison of broken dreams" to our "throne of destiny." All we have to do is believe in our heavenly dreams and let Jesus help us change our paradigms. This means we must find hope in our distress, encourage ourselves in the Lord, and reconnect with our zeal for life. In the end, our motivation for ministry will come from passion, not despair.

The Stephen Syndrome

Now, for the other side of the coin! How do we deal with the reality in Hebrews 11:39 that several men of faith died without receiving their promise? What do we do when there seems to be no chance for the resurrection of our dream? Do we continue to fight or do we throw in the towel? Also, is it possible that a greater purpose is working in the midst of our despair?

Misfortune can sometimes be a blessing in disguise. Actually, it is in times of great despair that we learn to trust the sovereign grace of God. One can understand, therefore, why the Apostle Paul stated in Romans 8:28 **"...that all things work together for good to them that love God, to them who are the called according to his purpose" (KJV).** He was convinced that God is sovereign and arranges all things after the counsel of His will (see Ephesians 1:10).

Such was the case of another believer in the New Testament named Stephen. According to Acts 6, he was a man of integrity, full of faith and power. Because of his excellent spirit, he was chosen as a deacon and shortly afterwards began to perform notable signs and wonders among the people. He was undoubtedly a rising star in the first century church and perhaps one of the best models for New Testament ministry.

Tragically, Stephen was killed before he reached the fullness of his destiny. Acts 6 and 7 record that a group of religious leaders from the synagogue of the Libertines were angered by his defense of the gospel and shook their fists in rage. Shortly afterward, they cast him out of the city and stoned him to death.

According to Acts 8, Stephen's death was a devastating blow for believers in Jerusalem. The fledgling church was already suffering under the strain of great persecution; now God's promise seemed to be dead, and they were burying a piece of their hopes and dreams. Bewildered by the event, devout men carried Stephen to his burial and made great lamentation over him.

During this time of mourning, however, something extraordinary began to happen. A disciple named Philip left the grief-stricken church in Jerusalem and went to the city of Samaria. As he preached Christ to the Samaritans, he began to experience the same caliber of miracles that were performed through Stephen. The lame walked, the sick were healed, and many possessed with unclean spirits were delivered. Eventually, the whole city was overcome with joy (see Acts 8:5-25).

What can we learn from this incredible story? Sometimes we have to bury our "fallen Stephens" in hope that God will raise up an alternative plan. When plan A dies, we must believe that plan B or C is also a part of the big picture. We must also believe that the last often becomes the first in God's kingdom. This means, of course, that we have to stop grieving over our failures and be willing to embrace something different than what we conceived in the beginning. When we make this connection, we will find a "Philip" waiting at the grave of our "Stephen." When the burial process is complete, this Philip will intuitively pick up Stephen's mandate for ministry and go forward with a fresh anointing.

Closing Thoughts

The question remains: Do we hope against all hope for the resurrection of our Stephen? Or, do we bury our Stephen and trust God to raise up a Philip in his place?

Paul tells us in Philippians 2:12 that each of us must **"work out your own salvation with fear and trembling."** The solution, therefore, lies with you and your relationship with the Holy Spirit. You must ask the Lord to show you what season of growth is upon your life. Should you hang on to the initial plan a little longer, or is it time to shift?

If the latter is true, then we must be willing to embrace seasons of transition, even though they appear to be difficult at the time. Like Peter, Joseph, and Philip, we must make the critical shift from our grave of disappointment to the joy that is set before us—no matter what form it takes. Otherwise, revival is delayed while men and women of God learn to shift.

QUESTIONS TO CONSIDER

- Have I let hardship destroy my hopes and dreams? In what way?

- Is it time to believe for my dream, or is it time to shift to an alternate plan? If so, what is the plan?

- Is the pain of my present condition greater than the pain it will take to change? If so, how do I shift from despair to hope in Christ?

SCRIPTURES TO PONDER

Now may the God of hope fill you with all joy and peace...(Romans 15:13).

And we know that God causes all things to work together for good to those who love God... (Romans 8:28).

Consider it all joy, my brethren, when you encounter various trials (James 1:2).

4
LIFESTYLE SHIFT

> **You Know You Are Fishing From the Wrong Side of the Boat When You Are so Driven to Succeed That You Have No Time for Rest**

Simon Peter said to them, "I am going fishing . . . ." They went out, and got into the boat; and that night they caught nothing (John 21:3).

Once we make the decision in our mind to shift, we are then confronted with other changes vital to our success. Some of these changes are spiritual in nature; others have to do with the more ordinary aspects of life. All are important to the fulfillment of our destiny and must be treated with extreme care.

In this chapter, I will begin with the issue of stewardship over the physical body. I suspect, however, that a great percentage of people who read this chapter will argue that the spiritual realm takes precedence over the natural realm. They are intensely focused on spiritual things and see no need to deal with such trivial issues as managing the human body.

Also, many fans of the King James Bible will contend that Paul warns believers in I Timothy 4:8 that bodily exercise profits very little. However, I do not believe the apostle was putting down stewardship over our bodies, but was making a distinction between the eternal value of natural things and spiritual things. When you read the whole verse in context, in other translations of the Bible, he is simply saying: Discipline of the physical body has some profit in this life, but godly discipline is even more profitable for this life and the life to come.

In spite of what the critics may think, therefore, we should never underestimate the role of how our physical well-being plays in God's purpose for our lives. In other exhortations in Romans 12:1 and I Corinthians 6:19-20, Paul implies that our whole body should be offered up as a dwelling place for the Lord. And, because our bodies are the temples of the Holy Spirit and the King lives in us, we are required to care for our bodies as one would care for a royal palace.

The Sin of Neglect

The story of Peter's weary night of fishing in John 21 raises many questions about this issue. According to verse three, he and the other disciples fished all night without rest or sleep. In spite of their weariness, they were driven by success at any cost to their well-being. When the morning sun dawned on their little boat, it was apparent their labor was in vain. They had nothing to show for their night of toil except weary minds and tired bodies.

Like these fishermen, many today are mentally and physically weary from the toil of life. Because of an unhealthy drive to perform, we have neglected the issue of proper stewardship over our bodies. Somehow, we have missed the fact that our usefulness to God is directly related to the management of our mental and physical well-being.

This reality is especially important for those who fail to recognize the critical link between the condition of their health and the success of their ministry. Many falsely assume that a healthy anointing can flow from an unhealthy source. This is especially true of those who believe that occasional manifestations of the Holy Spirit *in* and *through* their ministry can somehow compensate for the imperfections of a vessel weakened by neglect and abuse. As a result of this deception, believers often push their minds and bodies beyond the limits of human endurance.

Worse yet, many believe this abuse is a sacrificial requirement for an anointed ministry and often preach that the neglect of the human body is necessary to reach a higher status of spirituality. With great pride, these misguided ministries boast about their infirmities and weaknesses as though they are a requirement for receiving the anointing. They truly believe the weaker they become in mind and body, the greater the release of the anointing will be in their lives.

No doubt, the Lord uses human weakness to exhibit His strength. But too often, believers mistake the negative consequences of abuse as the dealings of God. In many instances, the Lord is blamed for our infirmities and the premature death that often follows.

Bodily Abuse

I am convinced it is not God, but mankind that puts our physical bodies at risk. Therefore, people who properly manage their physical bodies are given the best chance to live successful lives. Those who ignore this issue run the risk of premature death.

Sadly, I must admit that I fall into the latter category and have been an irresponsible steward over my physical health. Over the course of my ministry, I have abused my body with poor eating habits, insufficient rest, and lack of exercise. Until recently, I rushed frantically from one conference to another with little or no sleep. I ate tons of junk food after late night meetings and endured the weariness of chronic jet lag. On occasion, I ministered to the point of exhaustion and gave of myself when there was absolutely nothing left to give. Even when I was seriously ill, I would stand on my feet for hours and minister to people who were less needy than myself.

The outcome of this lifestyle resulted in several decades of declining health. I suffered from exhaustion, allergies, hyperventilation syndrome, anxiety attacks, irregular heartbeat, inner ear problems, fainting spells, numerous infections, hypertension, rheumatoid arthritis, partial blindness, digestive problems, ulcers, and a host of other complications that were directly related to the physical and emotional stress of ministry. All of this, I thought, was the price I must pay for the anointing.

Several decades ago, I began to suspect the twisted logic behind this philosophy and went to see a doctor about my irregular heartbeat. After running several tests, he said to me, "Sir, you are critically stressed out. Unless you slow down, you are a prime candidate for a heart attack." He continued to say, "I don't know what you do for a living, but it seems to be bad for your health. So you better stop before it kills you."

At that point, I was ashamed to tell the doctor about my occupation. I just couldn't bring myself to say that I was anointed to preach the good news of the gospel and heal the sick. After all, I was probably more in need of God's touch than anyone I knew, including my physician.

Shape Up!

Needless to say, the doctor's admonition drove me to my knees. I began to pray about my situation and asked the Lord to show me how I could avoid premature death. I was expecting Him to call me to a forty-day fast or an additional time of prayer and Bible study. When He answered, I was totally surprised.

"If you want to live and be a part of the next spiritual outpouring," He said, "you must get into shape." I was stunned, "Does this mean I must exercise, rest, and eat right? Doesn't the Lord know I am too busy doing His work to deal with such earthly things?"

At that point, the Lord revealed to me the importance of maintaining a healthy body. The implications were painful, but clear. My physical body is the dwelling place of the Holy Spirit and, therefore, must be a reflection of His glory. I was made to understand that a burned out and broken down temple cannot bear the anointing of the Holy Spirit any more than a house with faulty wiring can carry a full charge of electricity.

After thinking about it for a while, I began to see that the human body is incapable of sustaining the power of God on a long-term basis unless it is thoroughly fit and properly maintained. Actually, the Lord will withhold His anointing from our lives until we are able to handle it. This action is not the result of His anger, but His love and grace. Although He wants to use us, He is reluctant to risk His glory on an unsafe vessel.

Improper Stewardship

Proper stewardship of the physical body was seldom practiced by our predecessors. Historically, many men and women of God fell prey to this syndrome of neglect and suffered with poor health and died an untimely death. Even though they were extremely gifted, they were vulnerable to illnesses brought about by an undisciplined lifestyle.

It is well established by Bible historians, for example, that Evan Roberts, the leader of the great Welsh Revival, had emotional and physical problems which greatly contributed to the downfall of his ministry. He was known for ministering late into the night, sleeping two or three hours, and returning early the next morning to start the meetings. History tells us that he eventually suffered a nervous breakdown, which took him out of public ministry.

Also, William Seymour, the man God used as a catalyst for the Azusa Street Revival in 1906, died of a heart attack at the early age of fifty-two. Approximately three decades later, the highly anointed evangelist and founder of the Four Square Denomination, Aimee Semple McPherson, died at the age of fifty-three after suffering from tropical infections she contracted during her missionary trips abroad.

Kathryn Kuhlman, the woman who introduced the Holy Spirit to my generation, also died at the height of her ministry from complications following open-heart surgery. Also, Jack Coe, an extremely overweight evangelist known for his massive healing crusades, was diagnosed with polio and eventually died in his hospital bed at the young age of thirty-nine. Another famous healing evangelist, A. A. Allen, also passed away at the age of fifty-nine after a season of severe arthritic pain and liver failure. And, in my opinion, the recent deaths of other gifted men of God were partly due to the neglect of their physical bodies.

Why were these great patriarchs of faith and healing susceptible to the same diseases they cured in others? Why did several of them die an untimely death, even though they had raised others from the dead?

Sickness is the vengeance of nature for the violation of her laws. In order to minister effectually, we must obey certain decrees instituted by God. Again, one of these primary laws has to do with the way we care for our physical bodies. No doubt, the spirit is greater than the physical body. But, our bodies will eventually break down and experience premature death if we do not have the proper rest and nourishment. To avoid this tragedy, we must learn proper stewardship over our lives. If we do not make this shift, we are courting disaster.

Sabbath Rest

In light of the huge demands placed on the physical and mental health of today's ministers, many of us need to slow down and learn to relax. If God ceased from His work and rested on the Sabbath day, then we, also, must rest from our own labors and set aside regular seasons of rest.

Such was the case of a friend of mine who pastored in California. One month out of every year, he closed his church down for a time of rest. He instructed his staff and congregation to take time off to relax and enjoy their families. His philosophy was simple, but effective. If his church folded because of a need for rest and relaxation, then, in his mind, he did not want to be in the church business anyway.

In the end, my friend trusted God to sustain him during these down times. Without exception, God always provided financially for his staff and family. Also, many members of his church would return, bringing with them new people anxious to attend such an unconventional church. Although the church had a substantial congregation at the time, they began to experience rapid growth shortly after instituting the month of Sabbath rest.

Thanks to my friend, I am beginning to grasp the importance of proper stewardship over my body and soul.

By example, he taught me that in order to run with the next move of God, believers must make a major shift in the way we manage our lives. We need to have proper sleep, eat healthy foods, and, if necessary, take vitamins and minerals to supplement our diet. He also urged me to exercise my physical body and most importantly, to take the time to replenish my mind and spirit through worship and meditation on the Word of God (see Luke 4:42; 5:16; 6:12; 11:1).

Closing Thoughts

How does this play into the issue of coming revival?

In addition to the Sabbath rest instituted in the Old Testament, the New Testament also provides us with a perfect model for a stress-free life. As an example, Jesus possessed a divine destiny, but refused to be driven by a performance mentality. He was privy to the selfish ambition that many today misinterpret as passion for revival. He clearly demonstrated that the anointing is not attracted to anxiety produced by busyness and religious performance, but to a calm and peaceful spirit. Also, to maintain this level of serenity, the Lord often withdrew from the multitudes to a secret place of rest, where He spent time alone with His Father.

Does this mean we should examine the motives behind our work ethics? Are we to adopt the same ministry values modeled by Jesus?

In order to survive in the next move of God, it is necessary to confront the performance mentality that drives many of us to sheer exhaustion. We must also deal with the deception that more work produces more anointing. There must be a realization that true revival is not sustained by human might or power, but by the Spirit of the Lord. Most important, we must escape the strain and pressure of our hectic ministries and replenish ourselves in God's presence. Only then will we be able to make the shift from occasional seasons of renewal to a long-term encounter with God.

Finally, as I describe in the next chapter, a wrong performance mentality is a stumbling block to true revival. Actually, if I could add one more decree to the Ten Commandments, it would be "Thou shall not perform." Certainly, we must do our best to enter into God's rest. But once we are there, in His presence, Hebrews 4:10 says we must also cease from the sweat of human performance. This means all religious clamor must come to an end.

The author of Habakkuk 2:20 made it clear when he said **"...the Lord is in His holy temple. Let all the earth be silent before him."** In this regard, we have no choice but to shift from a performance mentality to total trust in His amazing grace (see Isaiah 41:1; Ecclesiastes 3:7).

QUESTIONS TO CONSIDER

- Is my ministry destructive to my physical well-being? If so, how can I change?
- Am I abusing my physical body, or am I treating it as a temple of the Holy Spirit?
- What must I do to spend more time with the Lord and enter into His rest?

SCRIPTURES TO PONDER

For the one who has entered His rest has himself also rested from his works, as God did from His (Hebrews 4:10).

"Come to me, all who are weary and heavy-laden, and I will give you rest" (Matthew 11:28).

"Take my yoke upon you . . . and ye shall find rest unto your souls" (Matthew 11:29 KJV).

5
PERFORMANCE SHIFT

> **You Know You Are Fishing From
> the Wrong Side of the Boat
> When the Fulfillment of Your
> Destiny Is Tied to Your Performance**

**...They went out, and got into the boat;
and that night they caught nothing (John
21:3).**

Like the other disciples in the boat, Peter was a
skilled fisherman. He was a professional and had
spent much of his early life casting a net into the Sea of
Galilee. It is my guess that he had a knack for fishing
and had learned certain techniques which produced
positive results. He needed no one to instruct him in
the art of catching fish or to tell him where to fish.
Fishing was second nature and he could cast a net in
his sleep.

On this particular night, however, Peter's attempt
at fishing produced nothing more than disappointment.
Regardless of his confidence in his own ability, he was
unable to lure one fish into his net. To make matters
worse, Jesus seemed to chide him the next morning
for his self-reliant attitude. Until this point in time,
the disciple had been fishing from a performance
mentality. Now, he was dependent upon the Lord to lead
him to success.

What were the underlying implications of this early morning encounter with the "resurrected Christ?" I believe Jesus was eager to show Peter the vanity of a self-reliant lifestyle. Because of the apostolic call that awaited this disciple, his confidence in self would have to be replaced by total trust in God. If he were to lead the church into a spiritual reformation, then there could be no room in his future for performance. He had to trust that God's ability was at work in and through his life.

Performance Mentality

When you look at the writings of Peter in the New Testament, it is obvious that the disciple had a dramatic shift in his life. In I Peter 1:2, he declared himself an apostle, not by his own works, but by the foreknowledge of God and the sanctification of the Holy Spirit. He was also able to say in I Peter 4:11, **"…if any man minister, let him do it as of the ability which God giveth; that God in all things may be glorified through Jesus Christ, to whom be praise and dominion for ever and ever"(KJV).**

In the coming revival, many of us will discover the limitations characteristic of a performance mentality. We will find that it is not about our ability to perform, but about the finished work of the One who laid down His life so we could be free from false expectations of performance.

This means we are no longer under the performance of the law, and we are free from its deadly curse. As stated in Galatians 3:10-14, we are now justified by faith in

Christ's performance, not by any performance of our own. According to Romans 11:6, if our righteousness comes by grace, then we can no longer lean on the performance of our own works—otherwise, grace is no longer grace.

To put it simply, there is going to be a catastrophic collapse of self-reliance in the near future. Every earthly thing we rely on will fail us. At the same time, a revival of trust in God will emerge, turning our focus from *our* ability to *His* ability. As with Zerubbabel in Zechariah 4:6, we will find that the success of our ministry is not by might or power, but by the Spirit of the Lord.

How do we make this quantum leap from a performance mentality to trust in Christ? Self-seeking men cannot advance the kingdom of God. Until they are broken by the Lord's hand, they are of little benefit to His purpose in the earth. This makes perfect sense when you consider that it is the fracture in a vessel that reveals the treasure within, and the crushing of incense that allows the fragrance to flow out.

Paul understood this paradox and stated in II Corinthians 12:9 that God's strength was made perfect in his own weakness. He continued this thought in verse ten, **"Therefore I take pleasure in infirmities, in reproaches, in needs, in persecutions, in distresses, for Christ's sake. For when I am weak, then I am strong" (NKJV).**

Obviously, Paul was not referring to poor stewardship of his physical body or to any moral weakness in his character. For the most part, his concern was centered on his inability to assist the work of God with performance and human genius. He was deeply aware of the futility of ministering in his own strength and also wrote in I Corinthians 3:19, "...the wisdom of this world is foolishness with God" (NKJV).

So great was Paul's revelation of human weakness, that the apostle declared the total sum of his earthly accomplishments as mere rubbish (see Philippians 3:8). In spite of his great ability, he seemed determined to exchange religious performance for humility that was wrought through brokenness.

Broken Leader

This reality was also true for another leader in Scripture named Moses. Other than Jesus, no man has ever equaled this prophet's ability to humbly carry the power of God. Like the Apostle Paul, he bore the glory of God, not because he was born humble, but because the hammering of God's dealings had shaped him into one of the meekest men on the earth (see Numbers 12:3; Hebrews 11:24-27).

According to Exodus 2, the process of brokenness was brutal, but unavoidable. There were, in fact, a series of devastating events which utterly crushed the prophet's self-confidence and drove him to total reliance on God.

First, this young deliverer who was educated in Pharaoh's palace made an unsuccessful attempt to fulfill his destiny. After observing an Egyptian abusing a Hebrew slave, he killed the oppressor and buried his body in the sand. But, once the deed was uncovered, he realized the futility of self-performance and had to flee from the wrath of Pharaoh.

As a result of this blunder, Moses spent the next forty years working in the desert as a lowly shepherd in the service of Jethro the Midianite. He had to unlearn the humanistic wisdom of Egypt and embrace a greater wisdom from a higher authority. Mighty Moses, the great scholar and heir to Egypt's throne, was now tending another man's sheep on the backside of a desolate wilderness.

In spite of his dilemma, however, the Lord had not forgotten the calling on Moses' life. When the fullness of time had come, the "broken prophet" found himself standing before a burning bush talking to God about his destiny. His commission to deliver Israel from their bondage of slavery was at last realized. As a sign of his calling, the Lord empowered him with a ministry of signs and wonders that would strike fear into the heart of Egypt.

Shortly afterward, Moses returned to the land of Egypt and began to demonstrate the power of God. Standing in Pharaoh's court, he turned his staff into a serpent and pronounced a curse of nine plagues upon the land. He also employed God's power to roll back the waters of the Red Sea, creating a safe passage for Israel to flee from the long and bitter tyranny of Pharaoh. At last, the Israelites would witness God's strength manifested through the frailty of human weakness (see Exodus chapters 7-14).

Reconstruction

Like Moses, many ministries today are about to have a head-on encounter with God. This is partly true because God cannot trust us to deliver people from bondage until we are first delivered at the burning bush of His presence. Before we stand in front of the king of Egypt to perform miracles, we must experience a miracle of divine brokenness that transcends our need for human recognition.

This means that the welfare of God's church is dependent on the maturity of her leaders. Throughout history, in fact, the body of Christ has suffered under bondage while the Lord dealt with the performance mentality of those called to ministry. Sometimes this process takes years. Other times it takes decades. Now and then, a whole generation will die in bondage because its deliverers are unwilling to deal with ambition and self-promotion.

In light of this problem, it is imperative that we submit our lives to the hands of the Master Potter. We must allow the Lord to break us, refashion us, and if necessary recommission us in a way more suitable for His purpose. If we miss this appointment on the potter's wheel, we are forever doomed to a life of mediocrity. If we make the connection, we will be transformed from glory to glory into the very image of Christ.

As a young preacher, this was a hard lesson to learn. After my ordination into ministry, I was more than eager to jump-start my destiny. I was motivated, ener-gized, and, most of all, determined to overpower the "dark side" with my gifting. On a daily basis, I paced up and down the floor of my prayer closet, racing my spiritual engines and rebuking the devil.

Fundamentally, there was nothing wrong with the desire to exercise my spiritual authority. The problem lay in my persistence to do it in my own strength and timing. I had no idea that I must be totally reliant on God in order to be useful to His kingdom. I also did not know that I must be broken and transformed into Christ's image before Satan considered me a threat. The reality that I was called by God did not mean that I was commissioned for ministry.

As you might expect, the Lord made it His business to shut me down and deal with my misguided ambition. Throughout the ensuing years, I found myself struggling to survive in an environment that was divinely orchestrated by God to break down my confidence in the flesh. Like Joseph, my heavenly dream was misunderstood by those closest to me, and I ended up in a well of betrayal and rejection. Shortly thereafter, I faced an even greater season of God's dealings that landed me at the bottom of an emotional and spiritual prison.

I still remember thinking: Is God trying to discourage me from ministry? Or, is my integrity being tested? At the time, I wasn't sure what was happening. As I look back, however, I can see I was not Christ-like and that my character needed extensive reconstruction. I have also come to understand the value of breaking, and now know that one of the constants of life is God's faithfulness to burst my balloon of inflated ego.

Actually, I am still baffled today at the unfinished work of the cross in my life, and I often brace myself for further assaults from heaven against my carnal nature.

Simply put, Jesus loves me, and He is faithful to work a greater weight of glory in my life even if it kills my flesh (see I Corinthians 15:31). Truly, it is not about my performance, but about His grace in my life. As John the Baptist stated in John 3:30: **"He must increase, but I must decrease."**

Scholarship Shift

Like Moses, many leaders today are well-trained in every aspect of life and religion. We can boast of the best seminaries and the finest theologians in history. Actually, most men standing in our pulpits are educated way beyond their predecessors. And, because of this impeccable training, we are equipped with an endless list of guidelines for building God's kingdom.

For example, we have mastered the mechanics of church growth, church management, and church education. We know how to evangelize our community, how to build a Sunday school, how to counsel the sheep, how to preach, and how to pray. Most of all, we know how to raise the funds needed to keep it all afloat.

Apart from the sovereign dealings of God, however, the schooling of man is often a hindrance to the cause of Christ. In my opinion, our past performances have not improved the spiritual quality of our lives or taken us to the next level of our destiny. Certainly, we know how to *have church,* but many of us have forgotten how to *have God*. As a consequence, we can be forever learning and never come to the full knowledge of truth in Christ (see II Timothy 3:7).

How then should we view the issue of higher learning? And, to what degree should we regard the importance of biblical scholarship? Although there is great value in formal education, many forms of religious training can provide a false sense of security. Again, the Apostle Paul states that we could be forever acquiring information, but never arriving at the recognition of the truth. He also indicated in Romans 12:2 that we are not to be conformed to this world, but transformed by the renewing process of the Holy Spirit in our minds.

If Moses had to *unlearn* the doctrine of Egypt, then so do we. If the Apostle Paul considered his religious knowledge as rubbish, then we must be realistic about the value of our own scholarship. Above all, we must realize that scholarship and performance are not necessary qualifications for service in the coming harvest.

Do I believe it is against God's will for people to attend seminary or other institutions of learning? On the contrary, I thank God for most of these institutions and respect their place in the church and the world. I am equally thankful for graduates of these organizations, who have chosen to give themselves to the church and the world. Their contribution to society is a living testimony to the value derived from the gift of learning. Honestly, I have the greatest respect for academics and the difference it makes in the advancement of our world.

Even so, the tragedy today is that many people attend religious institutions for the wrong reason. They make this choice, not because they are called of God, but because they are following a family tradition. Others pursue the ministry because they believe it is a noble profession and are infatuated with the respect that comes with being a member of the clergy.

The greater tragedy, however, is that a large number of these ministers often rely on years of training rather than on the Spirit of God. They wrongly assume that God will stamp them with His seal of approval just because they have fulfilled the required time in a scholastic institution. I wish it was that easy, but as a rule, the Lord is not as impressed with our training or charisma as He is with our brokenness of heart.

Closing Thoughts

Considering the lateness of the hour, the Lord is going to deal with the way we do ministry today. This means that all self-reliant ministries are coming to a swift end. Those called by God will find that ambition and performance are marked for destruction.

Whether successful, rich, famous, or poor, none will be able to escape this breaking and remaking of leadership. Like Moses of old, many of us will be driven from our comfort zone of performance and wander through the desert of God's dealings. As we stand barefoot in His presence, stripped of ambition and humbled before the fiery bush of Jehovah, all desire to perform in the spotlight will be burned to ashes. When the smoke clears, we will be free from a performance mentality, once and for all.

Also, as a result of this stripping, the way we minister will change dramatically. This is especially true for those laboring in areas they are not necessarily gifted for—especially leaders in positions of ministry that are not complementary to their gifting. As I will address next, Christians with misplaced giftings will soon be challenged by God to make an extreme gift-shift. When this happens, the church will be better equipped to make the enormous leap from self-appointed ministry to God-appointed ministry.

QUESTIONS TO CONSIDER

- Am I living my life from a performance mentality? How?
- In what ways have I let performance destroy my confidence in Christ?
- What must I do to get rid of ambition and self-promotion?

SCRIPTURES TO PONDER

"I have been crucified with Christ; and it is no longer I who live, but Christ lives in me; and the life which I now live in the flesh I live by faith in the Son of God..."(Galatians 2:20).

For it is God who is at work in you, both to will and to work for His good pleasure (Philippians 2:13).

So then it does not depend on the man who wills or the man who runs, but on God who has mercy (Romans 9:16).

6
GIFT SHIFT

You Know You Are Fishing From the Wrong Side of the Boat When There Is Maximum Effort and Minimal Results!

And He (Jesus) **said to them, "Cast the net on the right-hand side of the boat...." So they cast, and then they were not able to haul it in because of the great number of fish (John 21:6).**

In spite of the absence of fish in Peter's net, it would take divine intervention for him to see that he was overcommitted to the wrong spot. When Jesus raised the question of location, the weary disciple must have been embarrassed to be blindly fishing from the unproductive side of the boat.

Such is the case of believers today, who spend their time laboring in unproductive aspects of life. Like Peter, many of us have invested tons of effort into ventures that produce nothing but frustration and disappointment. This is especially true of leaders who minister in areas they are not gifted for. Like a rat running frantically on a spinning wheel, we often expend maximum time and effort without actually getting anywhere. The work is hard and long, and the payoff is of little consequence.

In spite of our misguided attempts to succeed, however, Jesus wants to make us better fishermen. As with Peter, we must make the decision to labor from the right side of life by hearing and obeying the Lord, not by trusting in the expertise of our skill or training. By no means can we continue to spend our time and strength on the same things that have never worked for us in the past. If we do, we will suffer the devastation of spiritual and physical burnout.

In my own life, I have exhausted myself with things that are not necessarily my primary calling. Not realizing my life was out-of-step with the core values of my destiny, I have majored on minor issues and minored on major issues. Because of my inclination to this deception, I have been unwilling to honestly evaluate my situation or take personal accountability for my misguided behavior. On many occasions, I misinterpreted my struggle to succeed in life as the opposition of the devil.

Consequently, I have lived a part of my life with a martyr complex—"just suffering for Jesus." As Balaam was indifferent to the angel of the Lord in his path, I, too, have stubbornly pressed through the opposition in front of me, not knowing I was resisting the divine intervention of God (see Numbers 22:34). On one occasion, I suffered one of the greatest setbacks in my ministry simply because I failed to recognize my limitations. In spite of repeated warnings from my friends, I made a choice to minister from the wrong side of the boat.

Right Thing—Wrong Time

It all began in 1993. Weary and tired of my hectic schedule as a conference speaker, I decided to stop traveling and start a church. The idea seemed logical. I had pastored previously and was well-known in the area for my prophetic ministry. What could be wrong with doing something as noble as pastoring the flock of God? Surely, the Lord would view this endeavor as a sacrifice for His kingdom.

At first, things could not have been better. Within two months, the church had grown from several dozen people to several hundred members. With a lot of hard work and prayer, I was convinced we would be a thousand member congregation within several years.

In spite of my optimism, however, Murphy's Law seemed to land right smack in the middle of the sanctuary. Everything that could go wrong did go wrong. Regardless of my best efforts, the whole thing began to fall apart at the seams. It seemed as though someone drove by and rolled a grenade of confusion through the door of the church. When it finally exploded, the result was horrendous.

After six months of ministry, five members of my worship team walked out on me, due to artistic differences and a series of misunderstandings. Fifteen or twenty other people, who felt called as intercessors for the worship team, followed shortly thereafter. Another group also left, not really knowing why they were offended. And, for reasons beyond my comprehension, several of my close friends walked away without saying a word. I never really knew why they left, except that one friend was offended because my car looked more expensive than his car.

Also, to add insult to injury, one of the primary leaders I was grooming to be my associate pastor fell into serious trouble and had to resign. Another elder got into a fistfight with a member of the church and was arrested and taken to jail. Several weeks later, two policemen walked into the sanctuary during my Sunday morning message and handcuffed a young man on a trumped-up charge of child molestation.

I also had to deal with certain cultural issues related to people living close to the beaches of Southern California. At the request of several older women in the church, I was prompted to send a memo to the young ladies doing interpretive dance in the meetings. The memo stated that all female dancers must wear a bra or remain seated during worship. The males must also dress appropriately and wear underwear under their walking shorts in order to be on the worship team.

This, too, caused a division in the church and sparked a heated debate on whether or not God looked on the outward appearance of a person or on their heart. Subsequently, another group left, offended by what they interpreted as pastoral control and legalism.

The final blow came when one of my elders informed me that he was going to take over the church. He told me that if I did not comply with his wishes, I would be out on the street. Eventually, I did have a church split and lost a majority of the remaining people. In less than a year, the congregation had been reduced to less than fifty people.

In an attempt to minimize the pain, I began to tease my leaders about writing a book titled, *Look Honey, I Shrunk the Church*. On one occasion, I even joked from the pulpit about doing a class on "Dyslexic Church Growth." The main topic would be "How to take your church from two hundred people to fifty people in less than a year, for no apparent reason at all."

In spite of my lighthearted approach to the problem, I decided to re-think my decision about pastoring this particular church. Like Peter, I discovered that I was expending maximum effort and getting minimal results. There seemed to be no choice other than to close the doors on that chapter of my life.

To this day, I still feel the sting of failure when I think about the mess I made while pastoring out of season. Since that time, however, I have learned the critical difference between the acceptable will of God and the perfect will of God. I know that good works are permissible, but I also know that the good can easily become the enemy of the perfect. Knowing this to be true, I no longer have the time or desire to invest my energy into anything less than the perfect will of God (see Romans 12:2).

Misplaced Gifting

In preparation for the coming move of God, we cannot continue to fish from the wrong side of life. We must put our effort into things that produce kingdom results and distance ourselves from pet projects that sidetrack us from our true calling. It is not only counter-productive, but foolish to spin our wheels in the mud of misplaced gifting.

If you are gifted for business or politics, for example, then by all means let God prosper you in the market-place. Don't let a religious spirit undermine your spirituality because you are not ministering in the pulpit. Remember that the kingdom of God is best served when you labor in the place of your gifting and anointing—even if that place is outside the church walls.

On the contrary, if you are called to be a pastor, then give yourself to pastoring, and don't be distracted by other ventures that might be unproductive to your calling. The same goes for itinerate ministers, evangelists, worship leaders, teachers, and others called to specific areas of service in the church. Put your energy into the area for which you are most gifted and beware of diversions. If you are not careful, you will get stuck in a quagmire of misplaced ministry which will drain you spiritually and physically.

What will be the outcome for those who are out of step with their God-given destiny? The last thing I want is to come across as insensitive. However, I must again emphasize that a major gift-shift is coming to misplaced ministries in the body of Christ. Believers laboring outside their zone of anointing will soon find the grace of God lifting from their lives. Many in the marketplace will end up in the pulpit. And, many in ministry will transition from the pulpit to the marketplace. In the end, the body of Christ will come into a season of effortless ministry. There will be minimum effort and maximum results.

Closing Thoughts

Someone once said that the pay is the same in heaven. I, too, believe Christians will be rewarded in the next life as a result of obedience and faithfulness to their calling, not because of their ministry status. The presumption that we will be better compensated because of our position of influence in the hierarchy of the church is unsupported by Scripture (see Matthew 20:1-16).

Actually, those in hidden places, devoted to doing the simple work of the ministry will fare just as well as the great patriarchs of the faith. Nursery workers, intercessors, businessmen, and others faithful to their callings will receive the same pay as apostles, prophets, and other governmental ministries. All will be compensated equally if they have been faithful to perform what they were called to do. On the contrary, those who have labored in areas other than their primary calling might find their reward to be less than expected (see Luke 22:26-27).

The bottom line is that believers must align themselves with the opportunity best suited for their gifting. I am also convinced that this alignment will completely alter our perspective of ministry and change our focus from *us* to *Him*. As presented in the next chapter, once we have made the vision shift we will see Christ lifted up as the focal point of end-time revival.

QUESTIONS TO CONSIDER

- Is my life and ministry performance-driven or grace-driven?

- Am I investing time and energy in an area I am not gifted for? How?

- Do I have a history of doing the right thing at the wrong time? How can I change?

SCRIPTURES TO PONDER

...we have gifts that differ according to the grace given to us... (Romans 12:6).

But to each one of us grace was given according to the measure of Christ's gift (Ephesians 4:7).

...whoever serves [ministers] is to do so as one who is serving [ministering] by the strength which God supplies... (I Peter 4:11).

VISION SHIFT

You Know You Are Fishing From the
Wrong Side of the Boat When You
Are Unable to Recognize Jesus
From Your Vantage Point

**But when the day was now breaking,
Jesus stood on the beach; yet the disciples
did not know that it was Jesus (John 21:4).**

There was something strangely familiar about Peter's
fishing trip in John 21. Several years earlier, he spent
a similar night of fishing without any success. According
to Luke 5:3-9, a local preacher named Jesus entered his
boat and asked the fisherman to thrust the ship out from
land. Apparently, an enormous crowd of people had gathered on the shore to hear the Lord, and He needed a place
to sit down and teach.

When the teaching session ended, Jesus turned His
attention to the problem of no fish. He instructed Peter
to launch out into the deep and let down his net. Bewildered by the command, Peter replied, "Master we have
worked hard all night and caught nothing...."

Nevertheless, Peter obeyed the Lord and cast his net
one more time. To his delight, the disciple caught so many
fish that the net began to break. Actually, the catch was
so massive that the fish filled two boats to the point of
sinking. In awe of this miracle, Peter fell down at the feet

of Jesus and confessed his unworthiness to stand in His presence.

Now, nearly three years later, Peter was reliving the past. Once more, he had spent a night of fishing and had come up empty-handed. He needed a miracle from God. This time, however, Jesus was not in the fisherman's boat in his time of need. Worse yet, Peter failed to recognize the resurrected Lord standing before him on the seashore.

Why did this disciple seem to be disconnected from the reality of the moment? Perhaps Peter was so consumed with despair that he had forgotten the earlier miracle. Or, perhaps he had lost hope that he would ever see the Lord again. Whichever the case, he was blinded to the presence of Christ in this season of his life. In spite of his past history with Jesus, the disciple could not identify the answer to his problem.

Reality Check

What is it about mankind that makes us forget so quickly? Why are some of our greatest successes followed by some of our greatest failures? There are several key answers. First, I believe that disappointment and discouragement can distort the reality of Christ's presence in our lives. In times of distress, there is often a sense of seclusion that drives us to a place of isolation. Once we are isolated, we are easy prey for the assault of the enemy upon our minds. Anger, fear, and unforgiveness give rise to bitterness of the soul, and this bitterness alters our perception of reality. Eventually, we are overcome with a case of spiritual amnesia and fail to remember the wonderful things Jesus has done in our lives.

I also believe that every mountaintop experience comes with a personal valley of disappointment. In Peter's experience, disappointment came on the heels of his greatest success. A few months earlier he was walking in the footsteps of Christ, performing miracles and casting out evil spirits. Now he was nursing the pain of broken expectations. Regrettably, Peter had given in to disappointment and had drifted far away from the One who called him into his destiny.

In my own experience, I have also made the critical mistake of losing my vision for the Lord. In the recent past, I have gone through difficult seasons of life and let hopelessness stifle my enthusiasm. At one point, I blindly ministered out of a sense of duty that required very little passion of heart. As a result, my motivation for ministry was reduced to mere mechanical reflexes.

Without realizing it, I was preaching because it was my job, not because it was my calling. In the end, disappointment clouded my perspective, and I fell into a state of spiritual blindness. Eventually, my boat drifted from its point of origin and I could no longer see Christ from my vantage point. I quickly discovered that **"where there is no vision, the people perish..." (Proverbs 29:18 KJV).**

Thank God I eventually made a commitment to set my gaze heavenward, and my spiritual vision was restored. Soon afterward, I made a vow to never again be sidetracked by the many distractions in life. I also made a quality decision to keep my eyes on the finished work of Christ. To this day, I frequently check my spiritual eyesight to see if my vision has diminished in any way.

Beholding Christ

There is an old proverb that says, *"You become like the thing you behold."* This means the things we gaze upon continually will be reflected in our countenances. In essence, what we visualize can so deeply affect our souls and spirits that we instinctively take on the mannerisms and likenesses associated with the images before us. If we focus on the calamities around us, for example, the misfortunes of life will be revealed in our faces. This is true of fear, failure, disappointment, and any other negative agenda that begs for our attention.

Our adversary recognizes this truth and knows that if he can get believers to identify with the many problems in our lives, we will take on the spirit of those problems. In all likelihood, this was on Paul's mind when he exhorted the church in Colossians 3:2 to **"set your mind on the things above, not on the things that are on earth."** The apostle knew that to become like Christ, believers must continually behold Him.

To this end, Hebrews 12:2 also indicates that we should steadfastly look to Jesus, the author and finisher of our faith. Although this is a much quoted verse today, I believe its origin is unique to Moses in the Old Testament. As described in Numbers 21:8-9, the children of

Israel had been bitten by fiery serpents and cried out for God to heal them.

Then the Lord said to Moses, "Make a fiery serpent and set it on a standard [pole]; **and it shall come about, that everyone who is bitten, when he *looks* at it, he will live."**

And Moses made a bronze serpent and set it on the standard; and it came about, that if a serpent bit any man, when he *looked* to the bronze serpent, he lived (emphasis mine).

Centuries later, we see a clear application of this Scripture in the New Testament. Speaking to Nicodemus about the salvation of mankind and His death on the cross, Jesus states in John 3:14-15; 12:32:

And as Moses lifted up the serpent in the wilderness, even so must the Son of Man be lifted up,

that whoever believes in Him should not perish, but have eternal life" (NKJV).

"And I, if I be lifted up from the earth, will draw all men to Myself" (NKJV).

And, finally, there is the ultimate vision shift in the writings of the Apostle John. He writes in Revelation 1:7 and I John 3:2:

Behold, He is coming with the clouds, and every eye will see Him...."

We know that when He appears, we will be like Him because we will see Him just as He is."

Practically speaking, if we are to live transformed lives, we must daily set our affections upon Christ. There must be a vision shift that redirects our focus from the earthly to the heavenly. As stated in II Corinthians 3:18, the challenge is to be **"...transformed into the same image from glory to glory, just as from the Lord, the Spirit."** Like Zacchaeus, who climbed up the sycamore tree to see Jesus in Luke 19:1-10, we, too, must elevate our vision. We must rise above the chaos around us and behold the Lord when He comes our way.

Visionaries and Blind Men!

In the Old Testament, the lives of both Samson and Samuel serve as examples for those called to great vision. One example is negative, the other is positive. In the case of Samson, God called the Nazarite as a deliverer in Israel and empowered him with an anointing to perform extraordinary feats of strength. According to Judges 16, however, Samson's vision began to shift from his calling as Israel's deliverer to an obsession with a Philistine woman named Delilah.

During a time of moral weakness, he revealed that the source of his strength was in his Nazarite vow to never cut his hair. Afterward, Delilah made him sleep on her knees and called for a man to shave off the seven locks of hair on his head. She then summoned the Philistines, and they seized the now powerless Samson and gouged out his eyes. Blind and stripped of his supernatural power, he was taken to a prison where he began to serve those he was called to conquer (see Judges 16:21).

In spite of his charisma and anointing, the man whose name in the Hebrew language means "sunlight" eventually died in total darkness. Sadly, his reputation as a great man of God was not able to save him from the blindness that was brought about by a life of compromise. More importantly, his tragic end serves as a warning for those unwilling to keep their vision centered on their heavenly calling.

In contrast to Samson, however, Samuel was extremely focused on his calling. He was in the greatest sense of the word a visionary. I Samuel 9:19 describes him as a **"seer,"** which in the Hebrew language means a "beholder of a vision." As a child, he was given incredible insight, and when he matured, all of Israel knew he was called as a prophet of God to the nation (see I Samuel 3:20).

Indeed, Samuel's life was an extraordinary showpiece of integrity. However, he was not only a great man of God, but this renowned visionary gave foresight to Israel in one of her darkest times. He prophesied the demise of Eli the high priest, and foresaw the rise and fall of kings long before they ascended the throne. Actually, his prophetic insight was beyond reproach, and according to I Samuel 3:19, none of his prophecies ever fell to the ground.

Equally important, Samuel never shifted his gaze from the purpose of God for his life. In every situation, he was faithful to walk out the vision given to him as a young man. And when he died, the great seer was so revered by the people of God that all of Israel lamented over him (see I Samuel 28:3).

Restricted Vision

Samuel was given vision because of his impeccable character; Samson was blinded because of his weak character. In many ways, a percentage of believers today are more like Samson than Samuel. Either they have compromised with the spirit of darkness and have been blinded by moral decay, or like Peter, they have let disappointment and despair crush their vision.

Whatever the case, many have drifted far from the origin of their passion and calling. Because of shifting moral values and spiritual indifference, there has been a negative vision shift, which has blinded believers to their God-given destiny. So great is this spiritual stupor that visually impaired believers often fall into a impassive state of existence and forfeit their right to maximize their lives and ministries.

Also, other believers have developed additional kinds of impaired vision. These limitations include a spiritual form of myopic vision, which produces a narrow-minded intolerance to the purpose of Christ in our lives. Tunnel vision is also prevalent among many believers and speaks of the inability to perceive the panoramic view of God's kingdom on the earth. Other forms of impaired vision, such as farsightedness and nearsightedness, also hinder a person's depth perception and have caused many to miss the mark of their heavenly calling.

Finally, in extreme cases, total blindness can be characteristic of whole congregations and denominations. Like Samson, a number of unsuspecting believers have been duped into trading their anointing for a yoke of spiritual blindness, which I am sad to say has destroyed their forward-vision in Christ. Especially troubling is the indifference of a few believers who are not deceived, but have made a deliberate choice to walk in spiritual darkness.

Closing Thoughts

How do we deal with failing vision in our own lives? Can our spiritual vision be restored to its original clarity? The author of Revelation 3:18 declares that believers who are spiritually blind need to be anointed with eye salve in order to see. The Apostle Paul also writes, beginning in Ephesians 4:18, that the blindness of heart which alienates us from Christ can be counteracted by a renewal of the Holy Spirit in our minds. He further states that this spiritual blindness can be reversed by putting on the new man who is created after God in righteousness and true holiness (see Ephesians 4:24).

At any cost, we must position ourselves for an extreme vision shift. Before entering the next season of revival, we must trust God to enlighten the eyes of our understanding and reveal to us the hope of His calling (see Ephesians 1:18). We must fix our gaze on Christ until such a time that we can behold His glory. Remember that we are truly blind until we can say, as did the author of John 1:29, **"Behold, the Lamb of God...!"**

QUESTIONS TO CONSIDER

- Have I let disappointment blind me to hope in Christ? How?

- Am I focused on the calamities of life, or am I looking unto Jesus?

- Do I have a clear vision of God's purpose for my life and ministry? If so, write out your vision.

SCRIPTURES TO PONDER

Where there is no vision, the people are unrestrained [perish] **(Proverbs 29:18).**

Fixing our eyes on Jesus, the author and perfecter of faith ...(Hebrews 12:2).

Set your mind on the things above, not on the things that are on earth (Colossians 3:2).

PART TWO

HOW TO KNOW WHEN YOU ARE
FISHING FROM THE RIGHT
SIDE OF THE BOAT

8
OBEDIENCE SHIFT

> **You Know You Are Fishing From the Right Side of the Boat When Obedience Brings You Into Full Contact With Your Destiny**

And He said to them, "Cast the net on the right-hand side of the boat and you will find a catch." So they cast, and then they were not able to haul it in because of the great number of fish (John 21:6).

Extreme purpose in God requires extreme obedience to God. This means the success of our tomorrow is in direct proportion to the depth of our obedience today.

Peter discovered the incredible power of this principle in one brief moment. Because he was willing to obey the command of the Lord, he was blessed beyond his wildest imagination. As described in Luke 6:38, he received an abundance of blessing **"...pressed down, shaken together, and running over."** Actually, his net was so full of fish that it was impossible to manage the catch by himself.

As with Peter, most major breakthroughs in life come about as a result of radical obedience. When we are obedient, a chain of events will come together, and like the pieces of a giant puzzle they create a picture of

God's benevolence in our lives. It may take a minute, an hour, a year, or a lifetime—but sooner or later the fruit of obedience will overtake us and blossom into a full-blown blessing.

It should come as no surprise, therefore, that every act of obedience is an investment in our future. Actually, these deeds of obedience have the power to position us for greater success in life, and in due time, they will lead us to the fulfillment of our destiny. As illustrated in Chapter One, every time we obey God we are skating to where the puck is going next.

For example, in the Old Testament David's obedience enabled him to defeat the many enemies of Israel. The prophet Moses also obeyed God and was empowered to deliver the children of Israel from a lifetime of bondage. Other men in the Bible, like Abraham, Daniel, Joseph, John the Baptist, and the Apostle Paul, were likewise known for radical obedience to the Lord.

Then again, disobedience is a cancer that eats away at our hopes and dreams, destroying any chance of success in the future. For example, King Saul disobeyed the word of the Lord, in I Samuel 15:26, and lost his right to the throne. Also, in II Kings 15:5, King Uzziah was stricken with leprosy as a result of his defiance. In addition, a wayward prophet in I Kings 13:24 paid for his disobedience with his life; another prophet named Jonah spent three days in the belly of a whale for a similar sin of disobedience.

The bottom line is that our destiny is shaped by acts of obedience and disobedience. Like it or not, the things we reap are often the consequences of our own actions. Because of Peter's obedience, he was able to catch a net full of fish. Because of Jonah's disobedience, the fish caught him.

Radical Obedience

Every major promotion in my life has come from personal obedience, not performance. In 1985, I relocated my family from Arkansas to Los Angeles in an act of obedience to the word of the Lord. I had no money, no home, and no place to minister. Actually, I knew only two people in the state of California and had not seen either of them for several years.

In the natural, the move seemed to be financial and spiritual suicide. It seemed unlikely to my friends and family that I could successfully make the transition. Furthermore, it was unrealistic to think I could immediately restart my ministry in a region where I was relatively unknown. So, upon arrival in Southern California, I took a secular job in the construction industry in order to provide financially for my family.

In spite of the challenges confronting me, I soon discovered the abundance of blessing that follows radical obedience. While praying one morning, the Lord impressed me to go to a neighboring suburb and prophesy over a pastor named Gary Greenwall. He had a large church in Santa Ana, which was about thirty miles from my home.

Reluctant to make the trip, I decided to call and see if I could give the word over the phone. When the receptionist answered the phone, I boldly asked her if I could speak to the pastor. She replied that it was his day off and he would not be coming into the office until tomorrow.

I hung up the phone thinking I was released from my commitment to obey God. "Maybe I didn't hear the Lord clearly," I mused; or "maybe I did hear correctly and the timing is wrong."

Once more, the Lord instructed me to get into my car and obey His voice. Again, I was reluctant to make the trip and reminded the Lord that I had visited the church only once and had not met the pastor. "It's just a waste of time," I protested, "and he is not going to be in his office anyway."

Still, I felt I must be obedient and make the trip. When I arrived at the church office, I told the receptionist that I was the man who called several hours earlier. I said, "I know you told me the pastor is not in today, but the Lord told me to come here anyway."

The young lady's face turned bright red. Clearly embarrassed, she restated that it was Pastor Greenwall's normal day off, but also admitted he was in the office taping his radio broadcast. "No one is supposed to know," she said. "He doesn't want to be disturbed by anyone."

At that moment I saw an opportunity to present my case. With as much confidence as I could muster, I said "Please go back to the pastor's office and tell him there is a man out front who says God sent him here with the word of the Lord."

To my surprise, the receptionist took off her telephone headset and walked out of the room without saying a word. In a few minutes, she returned and said, "Pastor Gary says you have five minutes and no more."

That was all I needed. I quickly walked to the pastor's office and introduced myself. With Pastor Greenwall's permission, I prayed for him and began to speak prophetically concerning the secrets of his heart. When I finished, he wiped the tears from his eyes and thanked me for being obedient. After saying our goodbyes, he asked me to leave my phone number with the receptionist on the way out.

Within three weeks, Pastor Greenwall called and arranged the finances to relocate me closer to the church. He bought me a new wardrobe, gave me expensive jewelry, and invested thousands of dollars into other aspects of my life. He also helped me restart my ministry, and he opened doors for me all over the West Coast. Before the year was over, I was once again working in full-time ministry. Because of my obedience, I began to experience a season of rapid growth.

The Seed of Obedience

As previously discussed, the spiritual principle of sowing in obedience greatly affects the condition of our present and future lives. In the incident with Pastor Greenwall, the blessing of obedience came quickly. At other times, the fruit of obedience has taken years, or even decades to materialize. In one instance, it took four decades, after my initial act of obeying God for the fruit of obedience to overtake me.

It all began at a Sunday morning church service in rural Arkansas. When I was six years old, the Lord instructed me to give the first dollar bill I ever made into the church offering. Being raised in a ministry family, I understood the principle of giving and receiving and assumed that my obedience would bring a quick hundred-fold return. I had visions of my investment returning to me in an abundance of one dollar bills.

For several weeks, I awoke every morning with an expectation of my coming blessing. Nothing happened, and the weeks turned into months, and the months eventually turned into years. To be honest, I was disappointed and a little bitter that the principle of sowing and reaping had seemed to fail me. By the time I reached adulthood, I had lost all hope of receiving a return on my investment and eventually forgot the whole thing.

Regardless of my lack of faith, the seed, which I planted as a small boy, finally came to maturity forty years later. One morning in 1998, I arrived at my Los Angeles office to find my assistant, Jerry Jamieson, with a big smile on his face. He handed me a check, which had come in the overnight mail from a total stranger. The amount of the check was fifty thousand dollars.

To say the least, I was elated that God would bless me in such a generous way. On the other hand, I was equally curious about the Lord's purpose behind the donation. Was the Lord preparing me for an upcoming season of financial leanness? Or was the money given to simply encourage me? To my surprise, the Lord whispered in my ear, "This is the return on the dollar you gave as a boy, plus kingdom interest."

Beginning that day, I found a new appreciation for the law of sowing and reaping. It became apparent that a seed sown in obedience to the Lord's command has the potential to produce an enormous harvest. It may take a period of time for the seed to reach maturity, but if we are patient, our obedience will eventually payoff.

The Rebound Principle

What does the principle of sowing and reaping have to do with the issue of repositioning ourselves for the next move of God? Every act of obedience and disobedience is critical to our future in God. This is partly due to a universal law which states that every action is counteracted by an equal or greater reaction. This principle was validated by Jesus when He declared in Luke 6:38 that the same measure you measure out will be measured back to you. Simply, the way you sow will determine how you reap.

In other words, to the extent that you are disobedient, an equal measure of negative fruit will begin to grow in your spiritual garden. On the other hand, if you are obedient, there will be an equal or greater return of blessing which will position you in a place of favor with God. In either event, the fruit of obedience and disobedience is cumulative and will eventually overtake your life (see Galatians 6:8 and Genesis 1:11-12).

For this reason, it is unrealistic to live lives of defiance and expect to arrive at our God-given destiny. In order to make full contact with our destiny, we must wake up to the power of absolute obedience and make the critical shift from defiance to compliance with God's Word. We must understand that extreme obedience is the spiritual currency used to purchase our future in God's kingdom.

It is also important to obey God even when it makes no sense, or when it seems unreasonable. If the Lord tells you to shift to the other side of the boat, then you must respond immediately. Like Peter, you will find that an abundance of resources awaits those willing to obey His voice (see Deuteronomy 28:1-2).

Closing Thoughts

It should be clear that believers desiring to see the unfolding of God's purposes in their lives should walk in agreement with His voice. Therefore, in closing, I am compelled to address two issues that have greatly limited our ability to shift into this place of radical obedience.

First, there seems to be an epidemic of distrust among many believers today. It's not that we are without motivation or lack a desire to be obedient; it's just that we often disobey because we distrust the Instructor and His instructions. Because of bad experiences in the past, we are conditioned to believe that God does not have our best interests at heart. Sadly, this deception has crippled our walk of obedience and prevented the Holy Spirit from guiding many of us into our destiny.

Finally, the fear of failure has also limited our ability to shift into a lifestyle of obedience. We somehow believe that if we obey God, there is a risk of getting hurt or looking stupid. On occasion, this may appear to be the case. But remember, it is better to obey God and bear the trauma of change, than to disobey and miss out on our future in God.

Also, as we will discover next, acts of obedience have the power to lead us into a place of financial blessing beyond our wildest dreams. Because of this dynamic, the Lord frequently demands irrational and illogical obedience, not because He wants to suppress our chance to succeed, but because He understands the incredible difference a change of direction will make in the outcome of our financial prosperity.

QUESTIONS TO CONSIDER

- Am I reluctant to take a risk, or am I living a life of radical obedience?

- In what areas of my life do I need to comply with the Word of the Lord?

- Is my future being shaped by my obedience, or am I currently reaping the fruit of disobedience? How?

SCRIPTURES TO PONDER

"**Behold, to obey is better than sacrifice, and to heed than the fat of rams**" (I Samuel 15:22).

"**In your seed all the nations of the earth shall be blessed, because you have obeyed My voice**" (Genesis 22:18).

"**See, I am setting before you today a blessing and a curse:**

the blessing, if you listen to the commandments of the LORD your God..." (Deuteronomy 11:26-27).

9

RESOURCE SHIFT

> You Know You Are Fishing From the
> Right Side of the Boat When There Is
> Access to an Abundance of Resources

Simon Peter went up, and drew the net to land, full of large fish, a hundred and fifty-three; and although there were so many, the net was not torn (John 21:11).

I f Peter had been disobedient that morning, the outcome would have looked quite different. Instead of enjoying success, he would have walked away from his fishing trip with an empty net. Yet, because he was willing to change his position and fish from the impractical side of the boat, the Lord prospered him greatly. There was such an abundance of fish that the disciple struggled to haul in the catch by himself.

Peter was no stranger to the issue of obedience. When he first encountered the Lord in Luke 5:6, the simple fisherman witnessed a similar miracle of provision. At the command of Jesus, he and the other anglers let down their nets and caught such a great multitude of fish that their vessels began to sink. Afterward, Peter fell down at Jesus' feet and confessed his unworthiness to stand in the Lord's presence.

In addition to these two miracles of abundance, Peter also witnessed the multiplication of fishes and loaves by Jesus in Matthew 14:19 and Matthew 15:34. In yet another miracle of provision in Matthew 17:27, Jesus sent the bewildered disciple fishing when he needed tax money. Right away, Peter found a copper coin in the mouth of the first fish he caught and was able to pay taxes for both the Lord and himself.

Not surprisingly, abundance seemed to follow Peter whenever he obeyed the command of the Lord. Jesus had called him to be a fisher of men in Matthew 4:19, and throughout the latter part of his ministry, there seemed to be no lack of fish in his spiritual net. On the day of Pentecost, for example, he let down his spiritual net under the inspiration of the Holy Spirit and netted three thousand souls for the kingdom of God (see Acts 2:1-41).

Money in the Fish

How do these things relate to the issue of abundance today? As indicated, fish in biblical terms are a type of humanity, and the fishing net is characteristic of the gospel of Christ. Equally significant, fishing represents the advent of global evangelism.

The problem today is that many churches have a habit of fishing in familiar waters. Instead of casting our net into the troubled waters of humanity, we continue to recycle the same fish that have been caught by other ministries. Consequently, with every fish we recatch, there is a temptation to compete for ownership. And, because there is a limited supply of resources in the mouth of one single fish, many congregations end up with recycled fish and depleted resources.

The good news, however, is that God has hidden the resources of the kingdom in the masses of unsaved humanity. This means we must step outside the walls of the church and redeem the unrighteous and the wealth of heaven that is in their hands. Jesus clearly said in Luke 16:9 that we are to make friends with unsaved men, which in my opinion enables us to influence them for Christ and share in the Lord's blessing on their lives.

Israel found this to be true when God instructed them in Exodus 12:35 to take ownership of the silver and gold in the Egyptian community. Again, the church of that day had to leave the comfort zone of their dwelling places and knock on the doors of the world. Surprisingly, the Egyptians opened their hearts and possessions to the Israelites, resulting in a huge resource shift.

How significant is this issue today? For those who might misinterpret this "resource shift" as presumption, I want to clarify several important points. First, it is not unrealistic or arrogant to take ownership of that which already belongs to our Heavenly Father. Haggai 2:8 indicates that every piece of gold and silver in the world is owned by the Lord, even that which is in the hands of the sinner. David also shares this thought in Psalms 24:1, saying **"The earth is the Lord's, and all it contains, the world, and those who dwell in it."** Revelation 11:15 further declares that the kingdoms of this world have become the kingdoms of the Lord and His anointed.

Next, the primary purpose of this shift is not about recouping the resources of the unrighteous for our own indulgence. It is about catching the sinner in the net of evangelism and replenishing the storehouse of God for the lean years that lie ahead. As Peter and Joseph were able to tap into a supernatural flow of wealth in time of need, we, too, will be given the opportunity to extract money from the mouth of the "big fish." Incidentally, the "big fish" can live in the business community, the academic world, or, as in Joseph's case, on the throne of government.

Partners in Destiny

I want to emphasize once again that we are going to see one of the greatest transfers of wealth in recorded history. Much of the world's resources are about to shift from the coffers of the unrighteous to the storehouse of the Lord. As previously indicated, the saints of God will take possession of the resources needed to establish the kingdom of God on earth.

How is this resource shift going to happen? What means will God employ to bring it about? There is a deep purpose of God at work in the earth, which I call the "great exchange." In His infinite wisdom, the Lord has designed it so the future of the church is dependent upon the world, and the future of the world is dependent upon the church. Because He desperately loves all of humanity, He has forced us to depend on one another. And in spite of our differences, our destinies are infinitely intertwined.

One can see this wisdom at play in the Old Testament story of Joseph's encounter with the king of

Egypt. According to Genesis 41, God troubled Pharaoh's heart with a dream that could not be interpreted by the psychics and wise men of his day. The Lord, in turn, had given Joseph the supernatural ability to understand the hidden meaning of dreams. In essence, Pharaoh had an abundance of resources, but no spirituality in his life—Joseph had the Spirit of God in his heart, but no resources.

As I see it, the Lord arranged a divine exchange between the wealth of Pharaoh and the spirituality of Joseph. According to Genesis 41:14, Joseph was released from prison to interpret Pharaoh's recurring dream. As a result, Pharaoh gave Joseph half the resources of Egypt and seated him on the throne of government. In God's providence the two men became partners in destiny. For the next seven years, Joseph stored grain in Egypt and was able to sustain the house of Pharaoh and the church in a time of great drought and economic calamity.

Marketplace Josephs

To this end, God is raising up Josephs today. These Josephs (male and female) are being empowered with both a spiritual anointing and a marketplace anointing that are unparalleled in history. And, whether or not they minister in the church or interface with the corporate world, the arts community, or other forms of commerce, one thing is certain: These marketplace ministries will have the intellectual and cultural grace to relate to society on a level unlike any ministry before them. Most of all, they will possess the divine ability of God to interpret the dreams of the unsaved and soothe the troubled heart of humanity.

Simply put, we are going to have a rare opportunity to infiltrate the kingdoms of this world with a gospel of supernatural power. Bear in mind, however, that Pharaoh did not come to Joseph—Joseph went to Pharaoh. Furthermore, it was Joseph who was required to change his residence and lifestyle, not Pharaoh.

I know this flies in the face of conventional religion, but the church in America must reconsider her approach to evangelism. Without compromising our values, we must become more culturally relevant. We must leave the comfort zone of that which is familiar and venture out into a sinful, hungry world that awaits a new breed of Josephs. If not, we will remain imprisoned in our religious institutions and never ascend to the throne of our destiny.

Also, it is important to know that our throne of provision is just a short distance from the prison. As with Joseph, God can take us from our "prison of poverty" to "throne of provision" in one moment. All it takes is a willingness to shift.

Closing Thoughts

During the course of Joseph's rejection and imprisonment, the Lord provided for his welfare. He could truly say as David did in Psalm 37:25, **"...I have not seen the righteous forsaken or his descendants begging bread."**

In the end, however, Joseph was happy to discover the vast difference between provision and blessing. He learned that provision is having enough—blessing is having more than enough. To put it another way, the Lord is willing to supply our needs, but He also wants to give us an overflow of resources—pressed down, shaken together, and running over (see Philippians 4:19, Luke 6:38).

As Joseph experienced God's miraculous wealth, we, too, are going to discover the Lord of extraordinary abundance. When that happens, we will not only be blessed, but become a blessing. We will make the transition from living lives of lack, to living lives of financial abundance.

This same dynamic of abundance also applies to the spiritual realm. Even though we are entitled to an abundance of financial provision, a greater inheritance awaits those willing to embrace the true riches of heaven. This spiritual inheritance is overflowing with supernatural gifts of the Holy Spirit and fresh manifestations of revival power. As we will see next, when we make the critical shift from religious rhetoric to fresh expressions of supernatural phenomena, we will create a spiritual legacy for the succeeding generations.

QUESTIONS TO CONSIDER

- What can I do to apprehend the full blessing of God?
- Am I content to be blessed, or do I have the capacity to be a blessing to others?
- Am I experiencing mere provision, or am I living a life of abundant blessing?

SCRIPTURES TO PONDER

A good man leaves an inheritance to his children's children, and the wealth of the sinner is stored up for the righteous (Proverbs 13:22).

"...and I will bless you, and make your name great; and so you shall be a blessing" (Genesis 12:2).

"I will surely bless you, and I will surely multiply you" (Hebrews 6:14).

10
PHENOMENA SHIFT

> **You Know You Are Fishing From the Right Side of the Boat When Your Catch Is Fresh and Alive**

Jesus said to them, "Bring some of the fish which you have now caught" (John 21:10).

There are a number of physical sensations familiar to most fishermen. One is the distinctive smell of fresh fish. The other is the feeling of a slippery fish, wiggling and squirming in your hands. Both are extremely intoxicating for a true angler and serve as inspiration to keep him coming back for more action.

It is my assumption that Peter and the other disciples shared this same enthusiasm for fishing. They lived and breathed the excitement of a fresh catch. People knew they were fishermen, not because they said they were, but because they smelled like they were. Their vocation was defined by the scent of fish on their clothes and bodies.

The same thing should be true of believers today. In a spiritual sense, we are privileged to carry the scent of our experience with God everywhere we go. People should know we are Christians, not because we have a Bible and go to church, but because we emanate His presence in every aspect of our lives.

Does this mean everyone will be happy with the way we conduct our lives and ministries? Perhaps not, but we should be excited about carrying the fresh aroma of supernatural encounters to the world, no matter how much they think it stinks, or how much ridicule we have to endure. When all is said and done, we alone will have to answer for the stewardship of the things God has given us. This is true of the gifts of the Holy Spirit and other supernatural manifestations that are unique to our spiritual experience.

Flopping Fish

Someone once said, *"You know you're in a fresh move of God when the fish are flopping."* The supposition is that the expression of jubilant emotion through a believer's life often indicates the presence of divine life within.

Contrary to this assumption, many churches in the Western World are not comfortable with emotional or physical expressions of their faith that could be considered fanatical. Although they love to reminisce about all the demonstrative manifestations of God's Spirit in the Bible, they seem reluctant to acknowledge the present value of these manifestations. Others will also affirm the authenticity of spiritual phenomena manifested in recent moves of God and yet downplay its significance in their church today.

In spite of this misguided mindset, however, the body of Christ throughout history has repeatedly experienced and expressed divine manifestations of the Holy Spirit. During the early years of Christianity, the church was alive with believers who expressed their faith in extraordinary ways. Not only was this true of the first century church, but other spiritual movements that followed thereafter carried the same DNA for revival.

The story is much the same throughout the last four to five hundred years. For example, in recent church history, a great number of mainline denominations experienced the phenomenal power of God in their meetings. Because of radical manifestations of the Holy Spirit, many Methodists, Presbyterians, Baptists, Congregationalists, Nazarenes, Catholics, and other such believers were at one time viewed as spiritual mystics and heretics. Regrettably, many were viciously criticized by their contemporaries and labeled as religious fanatics.

For example, in her autobiography in the mid 1500s, St. Teresa of Avila, a Catholic reformer, talks about fainting, swooning, and the inability to breathe or speak. Also, in the 1600s George Fox and his followers were given the name "Quakers" because of their extreme trembling and shaking during their meetings.

In the 1700s, John Wesley, the founder of the Methodist denomination also witnessed many of the same manifestations. He reported that people in his meetings would come under the power of the Spirit and cry, weep, roar, scream, laugh, tremble, shake, contort, and drop to the floor like dead people. Several of Wesley's contemporaries, including a respected theologian named Jonathan Edwards, and a great Methodist revivalist named George Whitfield, also reported it was common for people to cry out, faint, have convulsions, and fall under the influence of trances and visions.

Early in the 1800s, the Cane Ridge Revival that was spawned in Kentucky by a Presbyterian pastor named James McGready was noted for people crying out, shrieking, groaning, trembling, twitching, fainting, and falling down in joyful ecstasy. Later in that century, Peter Cartwright, another Methodist circuit rider and the great preacher, Charles Finney, who began as a Presbyterian and later joined the Congregationalist Church, reported numerous instances of convulsive jerking, spasmodic laughter, and speechless states of joy in their meetings.

Also, the Azusa Street Revival which began in Los Angeles in 1906, experienced unprecedented expressions of the Holy Spirit. This revival, which was initiated by William Seymour, the pastor of a black Holiness Church, was filled with such phenomena as drunkenness in the Spirit, shaking, speechlessness, holy laughter, visions, tongues, prophecy, healings, and miracles. Decades later, other moves of God also witnessed much of the same activity in their meetings. Much like the earlier renewals, most of these movements were comprised of people from every denomination.

Dead Trophies

Why the simple lesson on manifestations of spiritual phenomena in church history? Does the existence of past phenomena in the church set precedence for future revival? First, religious critics will tell you that manifestations of this kind are not harmonious with the character and nature of God. No doubt, a small percentage of the experiences previously mentioned are subjective by nature, but I still believe they are authentic signs that the Holy Spirit is among us. Also, the fact that such phenomena is not common to most believers today does not mean that they are not every bit in harmony with the Spirit of God and the Word of God. As any student of Christianity knows, spiritual manifestations are as old as the Bible and deeply rooted in the fabric of Scripture.

Second, I want to suggest there are only two kinds of fish—dead fish and live fish. In light of this reality, we have a choice to express our faith in a manner that is fresh and alive, running the risk of looking like fanatics, or we can play dead and quietly live on the reputation of past moves of God.

If we choose the latter, we are going to miss the incredible shift that is coming. Ultimately, we will settle into what I call a "trophy mentality." Our experience in God will take on the form of a lifeless trophy that hangs over the mantle of our spiritual house. Like the dead trophy whose life is long gone, all that will remain of our spirituality will be an empty shell of yesterday's experience, or at best, a mere conversational piece.

However, if we choose the first option, a deluge of fresh phenomena will overtake our lives. There will be an overflow of spiritual gifts, dreams, visions, trances, and other supernatural encounters. Times of emotional and spiritual ecstasy will flow from our innermost being like a wellspring of living waters. Our churches will no longer be "museums" where we worship lifeless replicas of things that used to live. Instead, we will live under the influence of "fresh wine" and freely partake of the intoxicating power of the Holy Spirit. The presence of spiritual phenomena in our lives will be the norm, not the exception.

Decency and Order!

Now for the critical question! Are we to assume that believers can experience extreme manifestations of the Spirit and yet maintain the appearance of decency and order? Can we have the power of God and respectability in the same church meeting?

Much of the church today is a showpiece for respectability. In many denominations, the new frontier for post-modern Christianity is defined by seeker-sensitive church meetings. The conventional wisdom is to protect the seeker from any possibility of offense.

To some extent this mentality is based on the Apostle Paul's admonition in I Corinthians 14:40 **"to let all things be done decently and in order"** in the church. Even so, when Paul talked to the Corinthian church about decency and order, I don't believe he was talking about the absence of spiritual life, or for that matter, the absence of spontaneity. Certainly, it was necessary to set divine order in the first century church. But in my view, such action was warranted because of the chaos created by people exercising their gifts simultaneously, not because he was trying to suppress the spiritual expression of individual believers.

In other words, the Apostle Paul implemented certain safeguards to curtail the eruption of spiritual phenomena so everyone could be used and heard. When he said, **"Let all things be done decently and in order,"** it was not a negative declaration, but a positive call to release people into their gifts and anointing. Again, the purpose was not to restrict the expression of the Holy Spirit through a believer, but to actually let all things be done.

Did the Corinthian church experience problems as a result of this exhortation? And, will there be negative fallout if we allow everyone to express their spirituality in today's church?

Perhaps, but like Paul, we should remember that the expression of spiritual life is often chaotic and messy, and consistent with the nature of creation. If you have ever witnessed the birth of a baby, then you know what I mean. The ordeal is usually loud, bloody, chaotic, and filled with emotional outbursts that defy decency and order as we know it. When the baby is finally born, there is a celebration of life in the room that has little regard for emotional composure or dignity.

Honestly, there is very little about our existence that is polite or proper—whether at our birth or during the formative years of childhood. In most cases, the sign of a healthy family is the commotion and buzz of life that is heard in the children. The same is true of a playground or a nursery. Constant noise is a sign that all is well. Silence and a lack of movement, on the other hand, are usually indicators that something is terribly wrong.

King Solomon said it best in Proverbs 14:4: **"where no oxen are, the manger** [stall] **is clean."** In the context of church life, the application of this verse is clear: We can have a neat and orderly church without the presence of life, for example, or we can embrace a nursery mentality that is somewhat messy, but filled with the sounds of spontaneous life. The choice is ours. Either we suppress our spirituality and remain unchanged, or express the creativity of the Holy Spirit and shift into greater dimensions of the supernatural.

Closing Thoughts

Considering the sensitive nature of this chapter, I want to make several things clear. As I have indicated, a great number of believers are about to make a dramatic shift into the realm of the supernatural. Having said that, we should not value spiritual phenomena above a personal relationship with Christ. This is true of spiritual gifts and other phenomena related to the supernatural. Any spiritual experience that undermines our focus to love the Lord, evangelize the world, and build His church should be carefully evaluated.

On the other hand, just because a believer's faith is not based on unusual manifestations or spiritual phenomena, it does not mean that it should be threatened by them either. Under no circumstances should we let the unusual nature of spiritual manifestations keep us from experiencing deeper levels of the Spirit. Bear in mind that the realm of the supernatural consists of a vast expanse of unexplored spiritual experience. And, the fact that most people are not accustomed to these phenomena doesn't diminish its authenticity in the least.

Also, since there is real evidence that these manifestations are biblical and have been present throughout the history of the church, it should come as no surprise that we are about to experience much of the same manifestations of past revivals—plus other phenomena yet to be documented. Certainly, we must exercise caution when dealing with the spirit world. But I want to emphasize again, that we cannot let the fear of unfamiliar phenomena keep us from coming into a season of fresh encounters with the supernatural power of God.

Finally, it is equally important that we impart the things we have received. As previously indicated, manifestations of the Holy Spirit are spiritual currency which must be given away to others. Also, as we will see in the following chapter, one of the greatest shifts we can make as a believer is the mental leap from: "It is all about what I can receive from God" to: "How can I make a spiritual contribution to others?"

QUESTIONS TO CONSIDER

- Am I living on past experience, or is my faith fresh and alive?

- Is my life too neat and orderly to accommodate spiritual phenomena?

- How have I let respectability keep me from a fresh encounter with God?

SCRIPTURES TO PONDER

"And it shall be in the last days," God says, "That I will pour forth of My Spirit on all mankind" (Acts 2:17).

...but one thing I do; forgetting what lies behind and reaching forward to what lies ahead (Philippians 3:13).

For the kingdom of God does not consist in words but in power (I Corinthians 4:20).

11

SIGNIFICANCE SHIFT

| You Know You Are Fishing From the |
| Right Side of the Boat When You Are |
| Willing to Give up Ownership of |
| What Is Rightfully Yours |

Therefore that disciple whom Jesus loved said to Peter, "It is the Lord." So when Simon Peter heard that it was the Lord, he ... threw himself into the sea (John 21:7).

It is one thing to share the spoils of success with others; it is another thing to give up complete control of all you have. As demonstrated in the verse above, Peter lost interest in his right to the catch after he recognized the Lord standing on the seashore. In biblical terms, he relinquished ownership of everything he had attained and threw himself into radical pursuit of the **"pearl of great price" (see Matthew 13:46).**

What motivated Peter to give up rightful ownership of his possessions and go after the ultimate prize? In my estimation, a series of past events brought Peter to this threshold of change. First, by all accounts in the Gospels, his earlier years of ministry seemed to be driven by self-importance and significance. According to Mark 8:32, he was so blinded by his need for recognition that he took the Lord aside and reprimanded Him for His predictions about the future. Jesus quickly rebuked the misguided disciple and reminded him that such presumption is demonically inspired.

Thankfully, after several years of living and ministering with Christ, Peter seemed to realize his bent toward selfish ambition. No doubt, he was impacted by the actions of a Savior who possessed all the legal rights belonging to a king, but also declared in John 8:50, **"And I seek not mine own glory..."** (KJV). Especially potent were other declarations of Jesus such as His exhortation in Luke 12:31—to seek first the kingdom of God instead of one's own rights. Once again, the Lord raised the spiritual bar for Peter when He declared in Luke 14:11, **"For everyone who exalts himself will be humbled, and he who humbles himself will be exalted."**

In my estimation, these words of Jesus probably had a great impact on Peter's drive for self-importance. This seems evident in the way Peter addressed the fading glory of mankind in his later writings to the church. At the end of his life, the now broken and less presumptuous disciple was able to proclaim that **"... all flesh is as grass, and all the glory of man as the flower of grass"** **(I Peter 1:24 KJV).**

All About Me

I, too, have been preoccupied with a struggle for ownership—especially in the area of personal significance. Tragically, as a young man, I was driven to make myself known among men. My focus was set on what I must do to get where I was going.

Certainly, I had a heart for people, and a burden to see the kingdom of God established in their lives. But to reach my absolute destiny, I believed I must first establish my authority as one called and anointed by God. I worked hard to take possession of everything I felt was rightfully mine. As a result, I invested an abundance of time into the development of my spiritual gifting.

As the years passed, however, my identity became dangerously tied to my accomplishments. Driven for significance, I drifted into a world of spiritual acquisition, where it became more about me than about Christ and His church. Without knowing it, I had given a greater part of my time and effort to building my own ministry instead of His kingdom.

It all came to the surface in 1993. While pastoring a church that was diminishing in numbers and finances, the Lord took advantage of my vulnerable position and disarmed me with one simple statement. Out of desperation I had been praying, "Lord what is going on with *my* church? Why is *my* church going through such a hard time?"

The Lord quietly replied, "The moment it became *your* church, it stopped being *My* church." At that point, the problem was unmistakably clear. Because of "my fish syndrome," Christ's headship of that particular congregation had been replaced by my own need for significance. Unintentionally, I had compromised in a way similar to Lucifer's original sin and exalted myself above the boundaries of my spiritual authority (see

Isaiah 14:14). In response to this revelation, I began to cry out, "Please Lord, deliver me from the sin of self-importance."

Significance or Contribution?

In answer to my prayer, the Lord has shown me several differences between the way sons and fathers conduct themselves. One of the most striking distinctions is their motivation in life. As a rule, sons are driven by performance and a need for significance, whereas fathers are primarily motivated by contribution.

The majority of young men, for example, are overly concerned about marking their territory through acts of performance. They work tirelessly to elevate themselves and have little room in their hearts to share the spoils of success with others. It is always about peak performance and the success of the moment. They often live for their own advancement, and are rarely concerned about the long-term contribution that is necessary to build God's church.

Also, those driven by a need for significance are reluctant to play by the rules. They have little tolerance for spiritual protocol and often take shortcuts through the path of integrity. Like Absalom, they give homage to their spiritual fathers, but are disloyal in secret. Given the right opportunity, they will sacrifice a lifetime of friendship for rulership. Consequently, men who are driven by their need to be "somebody" become one of the most dangerous threats to the advancement of God's kingdom.

True fathers, on the other hand, are motivated by the investment they can make in the lives of other people. They value the success of others above their own, and work to elevate those who are less visible. Their ceiling truly becomes the floor on which the next generation stands. Because they have been delivered from an unhealthy need for recognition, performance has no place in their hearts. These fathers are free from the stress of self-promotion and are content to let Christ perform His perfect will *in* and *through* their lives.

Ultimately, fathers live to give. This means fatherhood is attained when a man contributes more to his family than he takes out. This is true for natural fathers and spiritual fathers alike. In either case, a father does not require his children to provide for his welfare, but works tirelessly to nurture the dreams and visions of those under his care. In short, real fatherhood is defined by the investment made in others, not by the ability to acquire for himself.

Also, this investment goes far beyond financial provision and includes time, friendship, and other aspects of benevolence. Speaking about His own fatherhood, Jesus stated in Matthew 20:28 that He came to serve, not to be served. He also expressed in Mark 10:43 that the distinctive mark of greatness is the ability to give ourselves to others.

World-Class Fishermen

There is an aspect of fishing which also speaks to the theme of significance and contribution. It has to do with a method of fishing that distinguishes a world-class fisherman from a common fisherman. The concept is known as "catch and release."

A world-class fisherman, for example, fishes for the thrill of the catch and has no desire to take permanent ownership of the fish. After the fish is reeled in, he gently takes the lure out of its mouth and releases the fish back into its natural habitat. Although the fisherman has gained total ownership of the fish, he would never think of placing the fish in captivity. He knows if he lets the fish loose, it will grow and produce more of its kind.

On the contrary, the common fisherman is usually motivated by ownership. The whole sport is about the size of the catch. Even if he does not eat fish, his ego will not let him release the fish back into the water. In most instances, he will put as many fish as he can on a stringer and have his picture taken as a reminder of his success. The issue is not whether the fish live or die, or that anyone actually benefits from the catch, but it is rather a tribute to his fishing skills.

Catch and Release

Which is the proper method of fishing? Is it "catch and release" or "catch and restrain?" Before I offend both the spiritual and the natural fishermen, I want to make several things clear. I am not assigning a greater value to either technique of fishing. Neither am I suggesting there is anything wrong with catching, keeping, and eating fish. I am simply trying to illustrate a spiritual principle by using an everyday example of different methods of fishing.

Having said that, I do believe, in a spiritual sense, that the "catch and release" method is more in tune with God's end-time harvest than the "catch and restrain" method. Jesus clearly demonstrated this truth by the way He handled His disciples. After catching and training them, he quickly released them back into the world to reproduce God's life. The same was true for a demoniac in Mark 5:18-19, who after being delivered of demons, asked to follow Jesus. Like the disciples, he was also released by Jesus and commissioned to go back to his family and friends and testify about the great things the Lord had done for him.

Considering Jesus' behavior in these two incidents, it is apparent that the goal of the harvest is to catch and release fish, not confine them to religious boxes. The Lord seemed to be saying that it is more profitable to release one live fish back into the sea of humanity than to show off a whole stringer of fish. If this is true, then the challenge before us is to shift our thinking from a church mentality (catch and restrain) to a kingdom mentality (catch and release).

The late John Wimber, founder of the Vineyard Fellowship of Churches, exemplified this mentality more than any pastor I have ever known. He was determined to equip and release as many Christians as he could disciple back into the mainstream of society. Although meetings and conferences were high on his list, two of his main goals were to advance the kingdom through evangelism and to establish new churches.

Also, because of John's catch and release mentality, he had fewer church splits than most other Christian organizations. When an upcoming leader or group of people became discontented and wanted to leave his church, he would readily send them out with a blessing. Because of this approach, many who left decided to stay connected organizationally, and reproduced John's core values in their new church. As a result, the Vineyard movement grew to several hundred churches within a few short years.

Rick Joyner, another friend of mine, has also adopted the same fishing style. His motivation for having church is not to entertain lazy Christians or build the biggest congregation in town, but to equip and release an army of radical disciples into the marketplace. He recently told me that he was uncomfortable with fruitless Christians who sit in his congregation for more than two years, and he often prays that they will leave. He explained that they are taking up valuable space, and he needs their chair to equip someone else.

Like the late John Wimber, Rick also understands the incredible value of the "catch and release" principle. Actually, both men have refused, time and again, to define their ministry by the number of dead fish on their stringer. And, because they have consistently chosen kingdom principles over religious dogma, their effectiveness has been far-reaching in the world. In my opinion, this makes them world-class fishermen.

Spiritual Poverty

The same spirit of poverty that causes people to hoard money, and fishermen to keep more fish than they need, also drives many leaders to selfishly hold on to people. Throughout the years, I have seen ministers operate in a bizarre type of poverty spirit that masquerades under the guise of commitment and loyalty. Many of them expect believers to serve their ministry with unconditional commitment, but they are often reluctant to release them into their individual destinies.

What really is the bottom line for many of these leaders? I suspect the real issue is not that they possess a special revelation about commitment or that they need such a great number of people to survive. Rather, many of them are harboring deep insecurities and a lack of faith to succeed without the constant support and adoration of others. Ultimately, this mindset makes some of the greatest leaders cling to people in an unhealthy way.

Please don't misunderstand me. I am not saying that we minimize the value of commitment to our leaders; nor am I suggesting that we take lightly the issue of honor and loyalty. It is clear in Scripture that we are called to support the leaders God has chosen to train and equip us.

I am saying, however, that the mindset of the kingdom is quite different from today's philosophy of religion. Perhaps it was in this frame of mind that John the Baptist released his disciples to the ministry of Jesus. It is also conceivable that he knew Jesus would also give them away for the proliferation of the gospel, and send them out into the world to establish the kingdom (see Luke 9:1).

In this frame of mind, we must hold those God has committed to our care loosely in our hands. In our search for significance, we must not cling selfishly to things the Lord deems to be transitional and temporary. As I have amply stated, it is better to catch one soul and release it alive back into the harvest, than to have a large church filled with dead fish.

Closing Thoughts

In order to make the transition from significance to contribution, we must disconnect from old paradigms of thinking. Otherwise we will continue to preach a self-centered gospel that puts the emphasis on our right to ownership, instead of God's right to give away our disciples for His purpose on the earth. Bear in mind that the next move of God and the coming harvest are not about you and your ministry, but about the salvation of the world (see Luke 10:2).

Does this mean that we downplay the individual gifting of the Holy Spirit in our lives? Absolutely not! We all have extraordinary gifts from God that make us special. However, Jesus never said there was a shortage of extraordinary ministries—He said that the laborers are few. His prayer in Luke 10:2 was to send a body of believers into the harvest, to seek the lost, not their own glorification. In view of this, the ultimate challenge of the harvest is to learn to shift our focus from solo ministry to an army of workers. As we will see next, this shift is especially critical for leaders God has called to work together in the coming harvest.

QUESTIONS TO CONSIDER

- Am I seeking the Lord's glory, or am I seeking my own glory?

- Am I driven for significance, or am I motivated by the investment I can make in others?

- Do I hang on to people because of my need for significance? If so, what must I do to release them?

SCRIPTURES TO PONDER

"...the Son of man did not come to be served, but to serve..." (Matthew 20:28).

Let no one seek his own good, but that of his neighbor (I Corinthians 10:24).

A man's pride will bring him low, but a humble spirit will obtain honor (Proverbs 29:23).

12
LEADER SHIFT

> You Know You Are Fishing From
> the Right Side of the Boat When
> Your Success Is Greater Than Your
> Ability to Manage It by Yourself

But the other disciples came in the little boat, for they were not far from land, but about one hundred yards away, dragging the net full of fish (John 21:8).

With the exception of Matthew 17:27, Peter always fished with other people. When Jesus called him in Luke 5:5, he was fishing with several friends, who along with Peter, committed themselves to travel and minister with Christ. Even when the Lord took Peter up to the Mount of Transfiguration in Matthew 17:1, he was accompanied by his close friends, James and John.

Everything Peter seemed to do reflected the value of teamwork. Several days after Christ's crucifixion, for example, he was found in an upper room praying with more than a hundred personal friends and ministry associates. Also, his first demonstration of a miracle after receiving the baptism of the Holy Spirit was shared by John in Acts 3:1. Throughout the rest of Peter's life, he often co-labored with other apostles and prophets in the New Testament Church.

What was the inspiration behind Peter's fondness for teamwork? I believe Peter's experience as a commercial fisherman had taught him the value of working with others. It is also plausible that he was impacted by the many examples of Jesus' partnership with His Father—especially the Lord's declaration in John 5:19 that He could do nothing by Himself. In any event, the apostle was a team player who specialized in fishing for the souls of men. Speaking of his ministry with the other disciples, he writes in II Peter 1:16 that "**...we made known to you the power and coming of our Lord Jesus Christ, but we were eyewitnesses of His majesty.**"

Teamwork

Having grown up in the South, I learned to appreciate various kinds of fishing. There was bank fishing, trotline fishing, noodling, gigging, trolling, yo-yo fishing, and other techniques too numerous to mention. Occasionally, I would shoot at fish with a gun, or bow and arrow, or use cherry bombs to blow them out of the water.

Yet, my favorite method of fishing as a boy was bank fishing. I preferred the simplicity of solitary fishing with a rod and reel and a bucket of worms. Many were the days I sat on my bucket at the edge of a lake patiently waiting for a hungry fish to swim by and bite my hook. Although I greatly enjoyed the experience, my success was usually limited to a small number of fish.

At the age of sixteen, a couple of my friends introduced me to a more productive method of fishing. The technique is known by most Southerners as trotline fishing. For it to work efficiently, two of my buddies and I had to work together on the project.

The three of us would tie a long, heavy line with several dozen hooks to a tree on the bank of a pond or river. With the excess line in hand, we would cross the body of water in a small boat and tie the other end to a tree on the opposite bank. After fastening a heavy weight to the middle of the trotline, we baited the numerous hooks with worms and minnows and let it sink to the bottom. The whole apparatus, now completely submerged, served as an underwater buffet for hungry fish.

Once we were sure the trotline was firmly fixed, we returned to land and sat around a campfire anticipating the catch that awaited us. After several hours of enthusiastic conversation, we would jump back into the boat and set out to retrieve the fish that had taken the bait. One of us would paddle the boat, while the other person lifted the trotline off the bottom of the river and retrieved the fish, throwing them in the bottom of the boat. The third person's job was to re-bait the empty hooks as we moved along the trotline. On numerous occasions, we returned to shore with a boat full of flopping fish.

However, as I grew older and more confident in my fishing skills, I was convinced that I could handle the whole thing without my friends. One morning, I quietly sneaked away from my buddies and attempted to run the trotline by myself. Needless to say, it was a disaster! I lost many of the fish, nearly capsized the boat, and ended up with a hook in my hand. Humbled and a bit embarrassed, I returned to the bank with a newfound appreciation for teamwork.

Diversity

Jesus said in Luke 16:8, **"...for the children of this world are in their generation wiser than the children of light" (KJV).** I must admit that I have been somewhat offended by this statement in the past. Many are the times I have wondered what Jesus really meant. Was He saying that unbelievers were more intelligent than believers?

One day while watching a documentary about the success and growth strategies of large corporations, I began to understand the message of Luke 16:8. For the first time, I saw the core distinction between the mentality of the world and the mentality of many Christians. I realized that success in the church world is often measured by the *ability* to manage prosperity by oneself, whereas success in the corporate world is defined by the *ability* to manage prosperity through teamwork.

For example, companies such as McDonald's, AT&T, Wal-Mart, IBM, and other American giants, became mega-corporations because someone had the foresight to share the responsibility and profit with others. Without this foresight, they would have remained mom and pop stores, struggling to survive economically. Today, many of these mega-companies are merging in order to attain a greater corner of the market.

In this arena of life, the world is indeed smarter than most believers. While much of the church in America continues to divide into exclusive groups, with a single man running the whole organization, the unrighteous are consolidating people and resources to obtain greater efficiency and growth. They learned long ago that one person cannot effectively carry the sole responsibility of decision-making that is required to run a large company. In fact, every corporation that has a senior CEO also has a distinguished board to help make the decisions necessary to run the company.

Unlike the business world, however, most ministries in this nation have not made the critical shift from a "one man show" to "plurality of leadership." We boast about our spiritual freedom, but in reality, we still run our churches more like dictatorships than partnerships. The result is a spiritual and financial monopoly that limits the corporate growth of Christ' body.

In my opinion, this totalitarian mindset has set us back decades in the purposes of God. The top to bottom, pyramid style of leadership, which places one man on top to be served by those under him, is an affront to the teachings of Paul, the foremost architect of New Testament leadership.

Of course, we desperately need the leadership of apostles, pastors, prophets, teachers, and evangelists. Paul also made it clear that these ministries were given to lead as a team, bringing individual believers to the threshold of their destinies. Nowhere in the Bible does it indicate that a solitary ministry is set in the church for the congregation to support the leader's personal dream. Instead, plurality of leadership, which serves the vision and calling of each member in the body of Christ, is the mandate for true biblical leadership.

Perhaps this is the reason Jesus said in Matthew 23:9, **"and call no man your father upon the earth: for one is your Father, which is in heaven" (KJV).** Could it be that His concern was centered on the singular use of the word "father," rather than the use of the title "fathers?"

To put it another way, the Bible allows for spiritual fathers in the body of Christ, but discourages the idea that one single person (other than God) can serve as our primary Father. Thus, we are shown the distinction between a plurality of fathers (spiritual mentors) and the heavenly Father.

This mindset is consistent with much of Paul's writings in the New Testament. In I Corinthians 8:6, he talks about the one God who is the only Father of us all, but also used the term "fathers" in I Corinthians 4:15 when relating to a plurality of leaders in the church. In essence, he is saying that no individual can properly father a congregation by himself, but those serving as fathers in a plural sense, do share a collective responsibility to lead and nurture the church.

The Ultimate Team

In addition to the previous illustrations, there are numerous other examples of teamwork found in Scripture. In Exodus 4, for instance, God called Moses and Aaron to serve as one of the first ministry teams in the Bible. Although Moses was primarily the one anointed with miraculous power, he shared his rod of miracles with Aaron in Pharaoh's court. In many instances, their gifts were complementary, as they co-labored for the benefit of the whole. They were, in all aspects, an early prototype of the apostolic and prophetic teams which later emerged in the New Testament church (see Ephesians 2:20; I Corinthians 11:28).

In another example in Exodus 18, Moses' father-in-law recognized the limitations of his son-in-law's exclusive-leadership style and confronted him on the issue. Jethro urged Moses to appoint elders that could co-labor with him in leading God's people. Moses complied and Israel was able to make the critical shift from a spiritual monocracy to a more proficient model of team leadership.

How do these things relate to ministry today? We know we have reached a significant level of accomplishment when we need others to help us manage our success. Because the uniqueness of our gifts limits our ability to successfully manage alone, we must draw on the spiritual deposit God has invested in the church at large.

Several examples apply. First, as a general rule, prophetic people have a revelatory/diagnostic gift, which enables them to discern the secrets of people's hearts and pinpoint their specific problems and diseases. Even so, if the prophetic person does not possess the gift of healing, then the sick person receives a right diagnosis, but very little hope for recovery.

Likewise, those with a healing ministry are often weak in the diagnostic element of the prophetic, but have great faith for healing. Many times, I have watched them wrongly diagnose a person's illness, jeopardizing the sick person's chance for healing.

The same scenario applies to other ministries that face limitations in their gifts. This is especially critical for Bible teachers who are weak in evangelism skills and pastors who do not have a teaching gift. To effectively accomplish the work of the ministry, therefore, God made us dependent on each other. We have no choice but to value the unique gifts of others and to draw from the grace of God that is resident in their lives.

Closing Thoughts

To catch the next wave of the Spirit, there must be a dramatic shift in the way we view and administrate ministry. There must be less attention given to our self-reliant mentality, and greater focus on co-laboring with others.

In essence, if we want to facilitate the coming revival, then the "one man show" must come to an end. Actually, this outpouring will be so enormous that it will take the combined efforts of every man, woman, and child. If we continue to labor by ourselves, we undermine the purpose of true kingdom leadership, which is to empower every member of Christ's body for the work of the ministry.

On the other hand, we can become *one* as a body of believers, working together as a team, and not be *one* with the Lord of the harvest. As portrayed in the following chapter, it is also possible to build God's kingdom, and not build an intimate relationship with the King. Consequently, all that we do must first be founded on a bond *with* Christ that goes far beyond our ministry *for* Christ.

QUESTIONS TO CONSIDER

- How do I utilize the gifts God has invested in others?

- Am I a one-man show, or am I part of a team?

- What isolates me from co-laboring with others? How can I change?

SCRIPTURES TO PONDER

Five of you will chase a hundred, and a hundred of you will chase ten thousand... (Leviticus 26:8).

And He summoned the twelve and began to send them out in pairs... (Mark 6:7).

"...then you will know that I am He, and I do nothing on My own initiative..." (John 8:28).

13
RELATIONAL SHIFT

> You Know You Are Fishing From
> the Right Side of the Boat When
> Your Journey Brings You Into
> Fellowship With Christ

Jesus said to them, "Come and have breakfast."

... Jesus came and took the bread, and gave it to them, and the fish likewise (John 21:12-13).

Peter had a history with the Lord that was quite unusual. As discussed earlier, their colorful relationship began when Jesus hijacked the fisherman's boat and used it as a floating pulpit. From that time forward, Peter followed close behind, clinging to His every word. The impetuous disciple never seemed to miss an opportunity to demonstrate his zeal for God.

As seen throughout the Gospels, Peter frequently lived up to his reputation of boldness. In Matthew 14:29, he walked on the top of a stormy sea at the Lord's command. And in obedience to Christ, in Matthew 17:27, he went fishing and retrieved a copper coin from the mouth of a fish and paid the Lord's taxes. Even more daring, the disciple accompanied Jesus to the Mount of Transfiguration in Matthew 17:4 and attempted to dominate the situation, giving his bold and unsolicited advice.

No doubt, Peter was admired by the other disciples for his daring boldness. Even so, one could also assume he was known for his double-mindedness. He was a compulsive flip-flopper, who vacillated between two extremes.

In Matthew 16:16, for example, the disciple was praised for recognizing the deity of Christ, and a few verses later he was severely rebuked by the Lord for his forwardness. In John 18:10, he cut off a man's ear with a sword, not long after he and the other disciples were commissioned to heal the sick. And, in the most well-known example of double-mindedness, Peter was the first to pledge loyalty to Christ at the Last Supper, and the first to deny the Lord when He was later arrested and accused of heresy (see Mark 14:31; Luke 22:57).

Breakfast with Jesus

Generally speaking, Peter was temperamental, impulsive, and sometimes, just plain stubborn. In spite of his unstable temperament, however, I believe the disciple possessed a quality that set him apart from the masses. He truly loved Jesus! His devotion to Christ is clearly seen when he responded to the Lord's question of commitment, saying, **"Lord, to whom shall we go? You have the words of eternal life" (see John 6:68 NKJV).**

Years later, he once again answered the call of commitment to Christ. On this particular day, however, I am not sure if it was Peter's boldness or his colorful personality that attracted Jesus to him. In either case, the Lord loved him deeply. Of all the people Jesus could have invited to breakfast that morning, in John 21, it was impetuous, foot-in-the-mouth Peter and his band of brothers. They were a rough bunch of fishermen, but for reasons of His own, they were the Lord's first choice to share in His resurrection meal.

What was so important about this particular invitation to breakfast? Were there underlying implications for these disciples? As recorded in the Gospels, Peter and the other disciples had just endured a season of unthinkable tragedy. Only a short time ago they had accompanied Jesus to the Garden of Gethsemane, where He spent the night agonizing over the brutal death that awaited Him. Then, shortly after eating the Last Supper with Him, they witnessed His arrest, torture, and horrifying crucifixion.

Not surprisingly, Peter and the other fishermen had given in to a spirit of sorrow and defeatism. Knowing their pain, Jesus made a point to visit the grief-stricken believers after He had risen from the dead. Apparently, His purpose was to lift their spirits from the anguish of the Last Supper to the thrill of eating breakfast with the resurrected Christ. The Lord seemed eager to begin His eternal fellowship with the disciples and even prepared their meal.

Last Supper Syndrome

As with Peter and the other disciples, many today have developed what I call "The Last Supper Syndrome." A greater part of our identification with Christ seems to be wrapped-up in the agony of Gethsemane, or in the sadness of the Last Supper and the crucifixion.

To some extent, this is true of people who have not made the Romans 6 transition from identification with the Lord's death to identification with His resurrection. As a consequence, we live in the shadow of His cross without fully experiencing His glorious resurrection from the tomb on the dawn of that blessed morning in Matthew 28:1. Like the disciples, we have become so acquainted with the fellowship of Christ's sufferings, that we are not able to recognize Him in His present glory.

In spite of this negative outlook, something incredible is about to take place. A great identity shift is coming to the body of Christ. In the near future, Jesus is going to break through the dark night of our souls and reveal Himself as the God of our morning. As with the disciples, He is going to shift our vision from the heartbreak of "The Last Supper" to the joy of a "New Dawn."

How and when will this take place? According to Revelation 19:9, we have been invited to fellowship with the Lord at the marriage supper of the Lamb. Although this text deals primarily with the next life, it has significant implications for today. For example, Romans 6:5 declares **"...if we have become united with Him in the likeness of His death, certainly we shall also be in the likeness of His resurrection"** (NKJV). Practically speaking, we are buried and raised with Christ through water baptism, so we can walk in resurrection fellowship with Him in this life.

Be advised that a part of this shift will come about by a sovereign act of God—the other part will involve change on our behalf. As stated in Song of Solomon 4:6, we are required to pursue the bridegroom "**...until the day break, and the shadows flee away" (KJV)**. The Apostle Peter also states in II Peter 1:19 that we must embrace His majestic glory until the day dawns and the morning star arises in our hearts.

Right or Left?

In this present life, I believe we have an opportunity to experience the Lord as the bright and Morning Star of Revelation 22:16. I also believe that Jesus' sunrise appearance and fellowship breakfast with His disciples was a preview of the coming feast they would share in heaven. Earlier in Luke 22:29, the Lord had promised they would eat and drink at His table and occupy thrones of judgment in the coming kingdom. Now as a token of that promise, they were the first to dine with Christ after His resurrection from the dead.

It seems obvious to me that Jesus was grooming His disciples for intimacy in the world to come. However, the important question is: Can all who follow the Lord today acquire a place of eternal intimacy with Him?

The mother of James and John thought it was at least plausible. Speaking for all of us who desire to share the fellowship of Christ in the next life, she seized an opportunity in Matthew 20:21 to make a bold request of Jesus and urged the Lord, saying:

> **"Command that in Your kingdom these two sons of mine may sit, one on Your right and one on Your left."**

> **He said to them . . . "to sit on My right
> and on My left, this is not Mine to give, but
> it is for those for whom it has been prepared
> by My Father" (Matthew 20:21, 23).**

Although I am amazed at this mother's boldness,
I am even more astonished by Jesus' response. It is
interesting that the Lord did not rebuke her for what
many today would interpret as vain presumption. Nor
did He say that every believer would have equal status
in the next life. He made it clear that the position she
was seeking for her two sons was a valid request, but
would be determined by God at a later time.

The implications are staggering. In light of the
truth revealed in this exchange between Jesus and this
inquisitive mother, believers today should possess a
greater hope for our tomorrow. We should treat this
life as a dress rehearsal for the final act that is soon to
follow. Clearly, our level of fellowship with Christ in this
life has a direct bearing on our level of relationship with
Him in the life to come.

The Apostle Paul understood the gravity of this truth
and yearned for a greater identification with Christ. In
Philippians 3:11, he states his desire to attain to the
resurrection of the dead and writes in verses 12-14:

> **Not that I have already obtained it, or
> have already become perfect, but I press
> on in order that I may lay hold of that for
> which also I was laid hold of by Christ Jesus.**

> **Brethren, I do not regard myself as
> having laid hold of it yet; but one thing I**

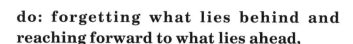

do: forgetting what lies behind and reaching forward to what lies ahead,

I press on toward the goal for the prize of the upward call of God in Christ Jesus.

In my view, Paul was not contending for his eternal security, but longing for a greater resurrection. I believe this is true, not only because the Lord has revealed it to me, but because it is supported by Scripture. Revelation 20:6 says **"Blessed and holy is the one who has part in the first resurrection . . . they will be priests of God and of Christ and will reign with Him for a thousand years."** The writer of Hebrews 11:35 also proclaimed that many great men of faith endured great affliction of body and soul in order that they **"...might obtain a better resurrection" (see Hebrews 11:35).**

Servants or Friends?

How does a believer make the shift from "mere Christianity" to a place of resurrection intimacy? More importantly, how does God determine who will sit in close proximity to the throne of Christ?

As stated, the degree of our relationship with Christ in the next life will be measured by the degree of our relationship with Him in this life. This does not mean that less connected believers are excluded from spending eternity in heaven. It simply means that we enter heaven on the same level that we exit this earth. Those living a life of lukewarm Christianity, therefore, cannot expect to have an intimate, passionate relationship with Christ the instant they walk through the doors of eternity.

Again, I believe the Apostle Paul understood the ramifications of this spiritual dynamic and cried out for something more than a successful ministry. Although he received incredible visions and had healed the sick and raised the dead, his heart was hungry for a closer relationship with Christ. In spite of his spiritual accomplishments, he cried out in Philippians 3:10, **"that I may know Him, and the power of His resurrection and the fellowship of His sufferings...."**

Is it possible that Paul had heard about Jesus' attempt to change the mentality of His disciples—from servants to friends? Or did he instinctually know that servants of the Lord are limited in their relationship with their Master, whereas friends share everything together? In any event, he seemed to understand the vast difference between ministry *for* Christ and relationship *with* Christ (see John 15:15).

Like Paul, I have also come to understand the significance of friendship with Christ. Due to a life-threatening illness, I was forced to make the transition from "servant of God" to "friend of God." While contemplating the possibility of death, I realized I was going to face a God I had worked for, but did not really know. Because of my ambition to build a ministry, the Lord had become more of a boss than a friend to me. Like Peter, I was blinded from the One that loved me the most.

Thankfully, I recovered from the illness and made some dramatic changes deep within my heart and soul. The first was a shift of priorities. I made a vow to never again place ministry over intimacy with Christ. I also committed myself to a life of passionate pursuit of the bridegroom. Regardless of the cost, I was determined to know Jesus in the fellowship of His resurrection. Much like the Shulamite bride in Song of Solomon 5:8, my heart began to cry out, **"If you find my beloved . . . tell Him I am lovesick!"** (NKJV)

Knowing Him

Christianity is much more than good church meetings. To a large extent, the Christian faith transcends preaching, teaching, miracles, prophecy, and other spiritual dynamics. In fact, Christianity is not an event at all—it is the Person of Christ. And, when we are friends with this Person, then the attributes of Christianity become a by-product of that relationship. In the end, the prize is to hear the Lord say **"Well done, good and faithful servant!"** (Matthew 25:21 NIV)

It is also possible, however, to stand before the judgment seat of Christ and receive a less favorable report. Jesus described the scene in Matthew 7:23 and declared that many will stand before Him saying,

"'Lord, Lord, did we not prophesy in Your name, and in Your name cast out demons, and in Your name perform many miracles?'

And then I will declare to them, 'I never knew you; depart from Me....'"

Was the Lord saying that gifted believers could be eternally damned for a lack of intimacy with Him? I have talked to people who think this is true. But for the most part, I believe this passage deals with certain priorities and motives of the heart. I am also convinced that the emphasis of this Scripture is not about heaven or hell, but whether or not we are in relationship with Christ. I assume this to be true because the word **"depart"** in this Scripture comes from the Greek root, *choreo,* which means "to give space" and carries the thought of backing away from close proximity to a person or thing. Also the word **"knew"** is derived from the Greek word, *ginosko,* meaning "to perceive or to have intimate knowledge of another. It is closely related to the Hebrew word, *yada,* which is translated in Genesis 4:25 **"...and Adam knew his wife..." (KJV)**.

The sum total of Matthew 7:22, therefore, could be unofficially, but loosely paraphrased: "Step back! Get out of My space. We were never intimately acquainted. This particular spot is reserved for those who have relationship with Me."

What an astonishing reality! Like Peter, we are going to discover at the end of the day that it is not about how well we fished, but why we fished! What we become in the next life will be measured by our relationship with Christ in this life. In my view, this means we could spend eternity in close proximity to the throne of Christ or live forever in the outer courts of heaven.

Closing Thoughts

Regrettably, our assigned place of relationship in heaven could be occupied by others who developed a close association with Christ in this life. In light of this reality, we must ask the following questions: Have I spent my time chasing ministry, or have I pursued a passionate relationship with Christ? Is my goal to be known by men, or is it to know Him?

The answers are difficult, but crucial to our spiritual journey. As the Bible indicates, it is the blessed hope of the ages to become one with Christ. In all the challenges of the Christian life, the greatest accomplishment is to know Him and the power of His resurrection. Otherwise, we spend our lives in search of significance and build ministries and relationships that attract people to us, instead of the Lord.

Clearly, the ultimate goal is to be friends with Him forever. In light of this, we must make the shift from servant to friend—from ministry *for* Christ to relationship *with* Christ. If not, we run the risk of hearing the shocking words, "Back away from Me! I was never intimately acquainted with you."

On the contrary, those in the right relationship with the Lord will be given an opportunity to live in close proximity to God's purpose on the earth today. As I will disclose in the final chapter, friends of Jesus who are open to change can expect to participate in an unprecedented outpouring of the Holy Spirit in the near future.

QUESTIONS TO CONSIDER

- What can I do to build a better relationship with Christ?

- Does Christ know me as a servant or as a friend?

- Have I made the critical transition from ministry for Christ to relationship with Christ? In what way?

SCRIPTURES TO PONDER

That I may know Him and the power of His resurrection... (Philippians 3:10).

"...If you find my beloved, as to what you will tell him: For I am lovesick" (Song of Solomon 5:8).

"This is eternal life, that they may know You, the only true God, and Jesus Christ whom You have sent" (John 17:3).

14

RENEWAL SHIFT

> **You Know You Are Fishing From the Right Side of the Boat When You Can Behold the Glory of Christ**

This is now the third time that Jesus was manifested to the disciples, after He was raised from the dead (John 21:14).

It is no surprise that Peter was one of the first disciples to witness the resurrection glory of Jesus. I believe this was partly due to his insatiable hunger for intimate encounters with Christ. In all of his shortcomings, this disciple seemed to be addicted to the presence of the Lord.

Also, Jesus had previously informed His followers that they would behold His manifest glory. His prayer in John 17:22, was that the glory He had received from His Father could be transferred to His followers. The Lord later stated in Mark 9:1, **"Truly I say to you, there are some of those who are standing here who will not taste death until they see the kingdom of God after it has come with power."**

At last, Peter was experiencing these incredible promises firsthand. Now Jesus was standing before him in resurrected form, ready to reveal His kingdom. Not surprisingly, the disciple was overwhelmed with emotion and once again, abandoned his fishing boat to follow the Lord. On that glorious day, he led the way for those longing for the manifest presence of Christ. There was, in fact, a dramatic shift in the spirit world that provided an opportunity for all mankind to enter a fresh dimension of God's glory.

Spiritual Storm

As with Peter, the Lord intends to visit this generation with an outpouring of His resurrection power. As I stated in the "Opening Thoughts," I have anticipated this approaching storm of glory for some time and have tried to position myself for its impact. Overflowing with expectancy, I devoted a greater part of my early ministry to preaching and prophesying about the coming rain of the Holy Spirit.

After what seemed like an eternity of believing God for a fresh outpouring, I saw very few results, and I began to grow weak in faith. Then at the point of losing hope, I had a God-encounter in 1987, which radically changed my paradigm for revival.

One night as I lay in bed meditating on the things of God, an unusual phenomenon began to take place. It seemed as though it was raining in the room. I could smell and hear the sound of fresh rain falling all around me. Instinctively, I jumped up and ran to the bedroom window, but to my surprise the sky was clear and the stars were shining.

"This is strange," I thought, and lay back down thinking I had imagined the whole thing. Then in a flash,

I saw the Lord standing at the foot of my bed. Quoting from Matthew 24:37, He said, **"As it was in the days of Noah, so it will be at the coming of the Son of Man"** **(NIV).** He paused for a moment as though I should take note of this Scripture and continued to say: "Just as Noah received rain that was unprecedented in his generation, I am going to bring an unprecedented rain of My Spirit upon your generation." Then in a much stronger tone of voice He declared, "The glory of My presence shall cover the earth, as the waters cover the sea."

In the remaining moments of my visitation, the Lord further explained the nature of this spiritual outpouring. He explained that it would begin as a small downpour by the end of 1993 and develop into a great revival flood during the course of my lifetime. He also warned me that many would scoff in unbelief and disregard the possibility that He was going to do something new.

In spite of their unbelief, the Lord concluded, "I will shake the fountains of the deep and open the flood-gates of heaven. I will release a global flood of My Spirit that will impact every tongue and nation. Those who thirst for My presence will be drawn into the 'Ark of Safety,' where they will ride upon the crest of one of the greatest revivals in recorded history. The waters of revival will gradually increase until the mountains and hills (earthly kingdoms) are completely covered."

Partial Fulfillment

Over the next seven years, I began to prophesy about the coming flood. I prophesied that, as Noah was promised things he could not comprehend, we, too, have no context for the spiritual flood that is approaching. I predicted that the floodgates of heaven would open and that God would shake the ancient fountains of revival that lie deep within the belly of the church. I further prophesied that as Noah gathered every species of animal into the ark, we also are going to experience an ingathering of every nation and tongue.

Then in January 1993, the Lord released me to prophesy specifically about an unprecedented outpouring of the Spirit that would begin in the latter part of that year. I began by saying, "A sign will be that the nation is going to have one of the wettest years in the last one hundred years. It's going to rain in the Midwest. It's going to rain in California. This will be the flood of the century. It's going to rain, rain, rain—both in the natural world and in the Spirit world."

Like clockwork, the prophecy began to unfold before my eyes. By early spring, rains and mudslides brought great devastation in California. A short time later torrential spring rains poured in the Midwest, causing one of the worst floods in U.S. history. Newscasters in St. Louis were saying, "This is the worst flooding here in over one hundred years." Floods of the century were the talk on people's lips all across America.

So great were the floods in the Midwest that the Missouri River overflowed its banks and spilled into the Mississippi River. The merging of these two rivers, shortly thereafter, caused the Mississippi to change its direction in several places. This was also the fulfillment of an earlier prophecy by Bob Jones that stated, "Keep your eyes open for the 'great flood'...when the Mississippi River changes its direction, that will be the signal for the beginning of a time of visitation."

By the end of that year, an extraordinary outpouring of the Holy Spirit had broken out in Toronto, Canada, and later in Pensacola, Florida. The renewal quickly spread to churches in North and South America, Europe, Asia, and other continents. Even more remarkable was the great number of conservative churches that were impacted by this renewal. Many of them experienced unprecedented encounters with the supernatural power of the Holy Spirit.

Eye of the Storm

Was this outpouring, which began in the early 1990s, a fulfillment of the prophecy Jesus gave me about revival for our generation? No doubt, history will record this move of God as one of the great outpourings of the twentieth century. Even so, I am convinced it was just a precursor to that which is to come. The Lord specifically told me in 1987 that the spiritual outpouring of the 1990s would simply be a gentle rain that would escalate into a spiritual flood of gigantic proportions. He informed me that the best is yet to come, and that torrential rains of the Holy Spirit will eventually fall on my generation and the generation to come.

When exactly will this begin? In my opinion, the first wave of outpouring has subsided, and we are presently in the eye of the storm. A blessed stillness is now in the atmosphere, hanging like a cloud over the church. And, regardless of what many believe, this pregnant pause is not the work of the devil to discourage us, but the grace of God given to prepare us for the coming deluge. It is an incubation period for change—a divine moment in time given to set our houses in order.

One can only assume that the depth of the coming revival will be in direct proportion to the depth of our preparation. The question is not whether it's going to rain, but whether we have made the necessary shift to accommodate the coming flood. Any limitation we encounter will not be on God's side, but will be the result of our own idleness.

Synopsis for Change

For the reasons described, the following preparations are a brief synopsis of the heart of this book and are critical to the shifts and changes necessary to participate in the next move of God. I know I am running the risk of sounding redundant, but my hope is to provoke the reader to a place of positive action. Remember, it is one thing to acknowledge our need for a fresh encounter with God and yet another to actually prepare as though it will happen.

1. Accept Change.

Change is the great neutralizer of dead-end dreams and lost purposes. All it takes to realign us with our initial destiny is a simple series of course corrections. These adjustments are critical to our journey and often serve as a rudder that turns our spiritual ship in the right direction when we drift off course.

2. Embrace the Discomfort of Change.

Change is often the tipping point for fresh encounters with God. However, most people embrace change only when the pain of remaining the same is greater than the pain it takes to change. With this in mind, we must welcome change as our friend, not our enemy. Remember, no pain, no change!

3. Repent of Hopelessness.

Before we come into the next move of God, it is important to repent of hopelessness and despair. Most important, this repentance should result in a change of heart that will accommodate the presence of the Holy Spirit. It is unrealistic to think we can change the world with revival without first dealing with the paradigms of despair in our own lives.

4. Learn Proper Stewardship.

In light of the extreme intensity of the coming revival, great demands will be placed on our physical and mental health. In order to survive, we must make a major shift in the way we manage our lives. We must get the proper rest, sleep, nourishment, physical exercise, and relaxation our bodies require. Our usefulness to God will be directly related to the management of our mental and physical well-being.

5. Repent of a Performance Mentality!

God is not impressed with our performance, but with our brokenness of heart. Until we are broken and refashioned by the hand of God, we are of little benefit to the purpose of His kingdom. In order to participate in the next move of God, we must cease from our own labors and lean on the finished work of Christ. Otherwise, we will see the coming revival, but not have the ability to receive and release its power.

6. Let Go of the Past.

As indicated in Genesis 19:26, Lot's wife lost her place in God's purpose when she looked back to her former life. Like many throughout history, she was called to be part of a movement, but became a monument of caution to those yearning to live in yesterday's glory. Her life is a testimony to the futility of trying to move forward, while looking back in the rearview mirror of life.

7. Develop New Vision.

Many Christians have a vision for bigger ministries and greater anointing. Although there is nothing wrong with these things, we desperately need a fresh vision for revival. As Noah was moved by faith to prepare for the coming flood, we must expand our vision for an unprecedented encounter with God. We must accept no limitations or imitations.

8. Practice Obedience.

It is impossible to reach our God-given destiny without learning the value of radical obedience. As stated previously, extreme purpose in God requires extreme obedience to God. Also critical to our journey is an understanding that self-sacrifice and performance cannot replace obedience to the Lord. In every area of life, we must come into compliance with the voice of the Holy Spirit before we can fulfill the will of God in our lives.

9. Believe for a Resource Shift.

A poverty mentality is the doorkeeper to failure, oppression, discouragement, hopelessness, and other negative influences. For this reason, we cannot nurture a spirit of poverty and expect to live a life of kingdom abundance. At any cost, we must get free of our financial limitations and make the shift from mere provision to abundance—from being blessed to becoming a blessing to others. Only then can we truly say that the blessing of Abraham is ours.

10. Walk in Humility.

It is clear in James 4:6 that the Lord resists the proud and gives grace to the humble. Also apparent is the reality that God expects us to conquer the powers of darkness through humility that is wrought in Christ. In order to be exalted, we must humble ourselves under the mighty hand of God. Bear in mind that we are promoted by humility, not by performance.

11. Embrace the Centrality of Christ.

The next move of God will not be centered on a particular doctrinal theme or the demonstration of a spiritual gift, but on the person of Christ. If we do not make the critical shift from self-centeredness to Christ-centeredness, we will miss our opportunity to properly represent Him to a lost world. For this to happen, we must change our emphasis from our ministry to His ministry—from talking about Him, to knowing Him.

12. Prepare, Prepare, Prepare.

Tomorrow's success is shaped by our willingness to prepare today. This means that the depth of our anointing will be in direct proportion to our depth of preparation. The question is not whether there will be a great outpouring, but whether or not our spiritual well is deep enough to accommodate the coming rain. Like Noah, we must give ourselves to the issue of preparation long before the flood begins.

13. Brace Yourself for Global Impact.

Noah's flood covered all the hills and mountains, affecting every thing on earth. In the same way, the coming flood is going to radically change the landscape of our religious and earthly kingdoms. Soon we will be given the opportunity to shift our vision from an earthly perspective to a heavenly perspective. When this happens, we will ride the crest of one of the greatest revivals in recorded history.

14. Prepare for a New Era.

Any encounter with the Holy Spirit has the potential to take us into our God-given destiny. As Noah stepped out of the ark into a new dispensation of God's kingdom, in Genesis 9:1-3, we will also have an opportunity to possess the whole earth. When that day comes, we will make the shift from spiritual complacency to ruling and reigning in this life through Christ Jesus.

15. Get Ready for Global Harvest.

In the same way that Noah welcomed every living creature into the ark, the Lord is commissioning an unprecedented ingathering of souls into His kingdom. This coming revival will include every nationality, gender, and religious persuasion. All of humanity will be given a chance to experience the great outpouring of the Holy Spirit prophesied by the Apostle Peter in Acts 2:17.

Closing Thoughts

Someone once said, *"There is a spiritual river that flows from our soul to the throne of God. If we don't paddle against the current we will eventually end up at God's house."*

I also think it is impossible to embrace spiritual change and not get wet with revival. As implied throughout this book, those willing to reposition their lives and ministries are going to experience one of the greatest God-encounters in recorded history. When this happens, a tidal wave of supernatural power will sweep the planet, just as the waters of Noah's flood covered the face of the earth.

The result will be a dramatic shift in the way we encounter and host the Spirit of God. There will be an increase of divine visitations, supernatural dreams and visions, signs and wonders, extraordinary miracles, and a host of other phenomenal manifestations, which will ultimately draw multitudes of people to the Lord. In the end we will see an unprecedented ingathering of souls into the kingdom of God.

I also believe this flood will carry us to the head-waters of a new heaven and a new earth. Once there, we will be given an abundance of resources and a newfound authority to administrate the kingdom of God on earth. We will finally be able to say, "...the kingdoms of this world have now become the kingdoms of Christ and His anointed." Above all, we will have the awesome privilege of being *changed* into His image, from glory...to glory...to glory...to glory...to glory....

... We will not all sleep, but we will all be changed! (I Corinthians 15:51)

THE END

SHIFT TEST

Try to be honest and choose the number for each question that best describes you. At the end of the test, add up all the numbers for a grand total. The final number will indicate where you are in the "Change Graph" on page 174.

0 = Not at all

1 = On occasion

2 = To some extent

3 = Very much

4 = Most definitely

___ Do I feel an overall need for change?

___ Do I feel my present condition is worse than in the past?

___ Am I losing my focus of the initial vision Christ gave me?

___ Is it difficult to see Christ in the midst of my journey today?

___ Have I drifted from my original call or purpose in life?

___ Have I neglected to take care of my physical body?

___ Do I struggle with disappointment?

___ Am I disillusioned about life in general?

___ Am I disillusioned about my ministry?

___ Do I tend to stick to that which is familiar?

___ Am I afraid to take a risk?

___ Am I reluctant to think outside the box?

___ Is my vision limited to the temporal world?

___ Do I feel like I am the Lord's servant and not His friend?

___ Has hardship diminished my hopes and dreams?

___ Am I stubborn and inflexible?

___ Is my lifestyle destructive to my physical well-being?

___ Am I too busy for regular seasons of rest?

___ Am I too busy to spend quality time with the Lord?

___ Do I have a performance mentality?

___ Do I seem to be driven for success?

___ Am I laboring in areas I am not gifted for?

___ Do I feel out of step with my destiny?

___ Do I tend to resist change and transition?

___ Am I inclined to live in the past?

___ Am I given to selfish ambition?

___ Do I have a tendency to promote myself?

___ Have I lost sight of God's purpose in my life?

___ Am I focused on my mistakes and failures?

___ Am I inclined to commit acts of disobedience?

___ Is my life or ministry hindered by a lack of financial resources?

___ Am I content to be blessed, while others hurt?

___ Has respectability kept me from fresh encounters with God?

___ Is my life too neat and orderly to accommodate radical change?

___ Am I too comfortable for revival that might be chaotic?

___ Do I tend to isolate myself from others?

___ Is it hard for me to work with a team?

___ Do I look for significance and approval from people?

___ Do I need a closer relationship with Christ?

___ Is my dream or ministry the most important thing in my life?

___ FINAL SCORE

CHANGE GRAPH

Minimal Need for Change 0-40	Some Need for Change 41-80	Great Need for Change 81-120	Major Need for Change 121-140	Maximum Need for Change 141-160

Point of Interest

If you are unclear about your present state of being, you may not be honest about certain aspects of your life, and may answer the questions inaccurately. As a result, your need for change reflected on the graph could be greater or less than it really is. It may be beneficial, therefore, for someone who knows you very well to answer the question, or questions, that you are uncertain about. The way they answer these questions on your behalf will probably be more forthright, resulting in a more accurate rating.